Adobe®
Photoshop®
Elements 4.0

CLASSROOM
IN A BOOK®

Adobe

122095, 122094

Adobe®
Photoshop®
Elements 4.0

CLASSROOM
IN A BOOK®

w.adobepress.com

Adobe

Adobe Press books are published by Peachpit, Berkeley, CA. To report errors, please send a note to errata@peachpit.com.

Printed in the U.S.A.

ISBN 0-321-38482-2

9 8 7 6 5 4 3 2 1

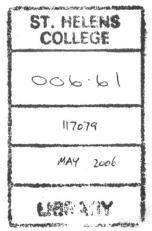

Lesson files . . . and so much more

The *Adobe Photoshop Elements 4.0 Classroom in a Book* CD includes the lesson files that you'll need to complete the exercises in this book, as well as other content to help you learn more about Adobe Photoshop Elements and use it with greater efficiency and ease. The diagram below represents the contents of the CD, which should help you locate the files you need.

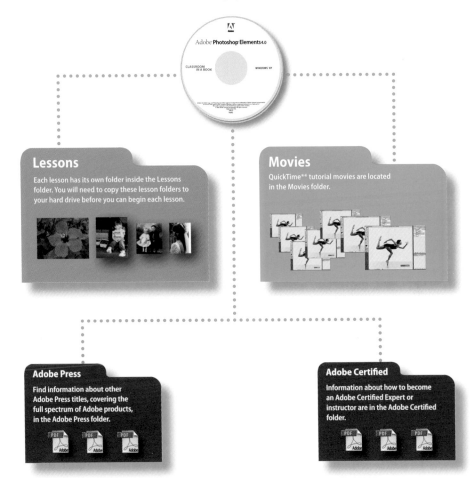

Lessons

Each lesson has its own folder inside the Lessons folder. You will need to copy these lesson folders to your hard drive before you can begin each lesson.

Movies

QuickTime** tutorial movies are located in the Movies folder.

Adobe Press

Find information about other Adobe Press titles, covering the full spectrum of Adobe products, in the Adobe Press folder.

Adobe Certified

Information about how to become an Adobe Certified Expert or instructor are in the Adobe Certified folder.

 *** The latest version of Apple QuickTime can be downloaded from www.apple.com/quicktime/download.*

Contents

2   Organizing and Sharing Photos

3   Sharing Creations

4   Adjusting Color in Images

5 Fixing Exposure Problems

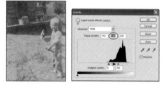

6   **Repairing and Retouching Images**

7   **Working with Text**

8   Combining Multiple Images

9   Advanced Editing Techniques

Getting Started

Adobe® Photoshop® Elements 4.0 delivers image-editing tools that balance power and versatility with ease of use. Photoshop Elements 4.0 is ideal for home users, hobbyists, business users, and professional photographers— anyone who wants to produce good-looking pictures and sophisticated graphics for the Web and for print.

If you've used earlier versions of Photoshop Elements, you'll find that this Classroom in a Book® teaches many advanced skills and innovative features that Adobe Systems introduces in this version. If you're new to Adobe Photoshop Elements 4.0, you'll learn the fundamental concepts and techniques that help you master the application.

About Classroom in a Book

Adobe Photoshop Elements 4.0 Classroom in a Book is part of the official training series for Adobe graphics and publishing software developed by Adobe product experts. Each lesson in this book is made up of a series of self-paced projects that give you hands-on experience using Photoshop Elements 4.0.

The *Adobe Photoshop Elements 4.0 Classroom in a Book* includes a CD attached to the inside back cover of this book. On the CD you'll find all the image files used for the lessons in this book, along with additional learning resources.

Prerequisites

Before you begin working on the lessons in this book, make sure that you and your computer are ready.

Note: The lessons in this book are designed to be used only on Windows 2000 or Windows XP.

Requirements on your computer

You'll need about 300 MB of free space on your hard disk for the lesson files and the work files you'll create. The lesson files are on the CD attached to the inside back cover of this book, and are necessary for your work in the lessons.

Required skills

The lessons in the *Adobe Photoshop Elements 4.0 Classroom in a Book* assume that you have a working knowledge of your computer and its operating system. This book does not teach the most basic and generic computer skills. If you can answer yes to the following questions, then you're probably well-qualified to start working on the projects in these lessons. Most users should work on the lessons in the order in which they occur in the book.

• Do you know how to use the Microsoft Windows Start button and the Windows Taskbar? Can you open menus and submenus, and choose items from those menus?

• Do you know how to use My Computer, Windows Explorer, or Internet Explorer to find items stored in folders on your computer or browse the Internet?

• Are you comfortable using the mouse to move the cursor, select items, drag, and deselect? Have you used context menus, which open when you right-click items?

• When you have two or more open applications, do you know how to switch from one to another? Do you know how to switch to the Windows Desktop?

• Do you know how to open, close, and minimize individual windows? Can you move them to different locations on your screen? Can you resize a window by dragging?

• Can you scroll (vertically and horizontally) within a window to see contents that may not be visible in the displayed area?

• Are you familiar with the menus across the top of an application and how to use those menus?

• Have you used dialog boxes, such as the Print dialog box? Do you know how to click arrow icons to open a drop-down menu within a dialog box?

• Can you open, save, and close a file? Are you familiar with word processing tasks, such as typing, selecting words, backspacing, deleting, copying, pasting, and changing text?

• Do you know how to open and find information in Microsoft Windows Help?

If there are gaps in your mastery of these skills, see the Microsoft documentation for your version of Windows. Or, ask a computer-savvy friend or instructor for help.

Installing Adobe Photoshop Elements 4.0

You must purchase the Adobe Photoshop Elements 4.0 software separately and install it on a computer running Windows 2000 or Windows XP. For system requirements and complete instructions on installing the software, see the Photoshop Elements 4.0 application CD and documentation.

Copying the Classroom in a Book files

The CD attached to the inside back cover of this book includes all the electronic files for the lessons in this book. The files will be organized using a catalog that is an essential part of many projects. Keep all the lesson files on your computer until after you have finished all the lessons.

Note: The images on the CD are practice files, provided for your personal use in these lessons. You are not authorized to use these photographs commercially, or to publish or distribute them in any form without written permissions from Adobe Systems, Inc., and the individual photographers who took the pictures, or other copyright holders.

Copying the Lessons files from the CD

1   Insert the *Adobe Photoshop Elements 4.0 Classroom in a Book* CD in your CD-ROM drive. If a message appears asking what you want Windows to do, select Open Folder to View Files Using Windows Explorer, and click OK.

If no message appears, open My Computer and double-click the CD icon to open it.

2   Locate the Lessons folder on the CD and copy it to the My Documents folder on your computer.

3   When your computer finishes copying the Lessons file, remove the CD from your CD-ROM drive and put it away.

Go to the procedure on the next page before you start the lessons.

Creating a work folder

You'll want to create a folder where you can save all of your work as you complete the lessons in this book. You'll use this folder in many of the lessons.

1   In Windows Explorer open the Lessons folder that you copied to the My Documents folder on your hard drive.

2   In the Lessons folder choose File > New > Folder. A new folder is created in the Lessons folder. Type **My CIB Work** to name the folder.

Creating a catalog

You'll use a catalog to organize the image files for the lessons in this book. This keeps all your images together in one easy-to-access location. You'll use the process of importing files into a catalog whenever you need to import images into Photoshop Elements from your digital camera, or import images already stored on your hard drive.

1   Start Adobe Photoshop Elements 4.0. In the Photoshop Elements Welcome Screen, choose View and Organize Photos. This starts Photoshop Elements in the Organizer mode.

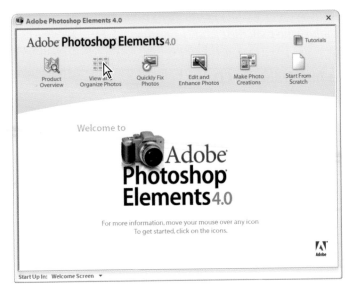

Note: *If this is the first time you have started the Organizer, an alert message may appear asking if you would like to specify the location of photos. Click No if this alert message appears.*

2   Choose File > Catalog and in the Catalog window that opens, click the New button. Enter the file name **CIB Catalog** and then click the Save button.

Note: *Do not change the location of where the Catalog file is stored.*

3   Choose File > Get Photos > From Files and Folders. In the Get Photos from Files and Folders window, open the My Documents folder. Click only once to select the Lessons folder that you copied from the CD. Do not double-click, as you do not want to open the Lessons folder.

4   Set the following options in the Get Photos from Files and Folders window:

• Confirm that the Get Photos from Subfolders checkbox is selected in the lower right corner of the window.

• Deselect the Automatically Fix Red Eyes option. This is a great option that you will learn more about as you work through the lessons, but we won't use it just yet. Click the Get Photos button. A window will open showing the photos being imported.

5   The Import Attached Tags window opens. Click the Select All button, and then click the OK button. The images you are bringing into the catalog contain additional information, known as tags, that will help you organize them as you proceed through the book. We've added these tags to help make it easier to work with the lessons in this book. You'll learn all about tags in Lesson 2.

After the image files are imported into the catalog, the tags are displayed along the right side of the display. The tags will be referenced in the lessons throughout this book.

6   Photoshop Elements may display a dialog box, informing you that the only items displayed in the Organizer are those you just imported. If an alert is displayed, click OK to close this window. Click the Back to All Photos button.

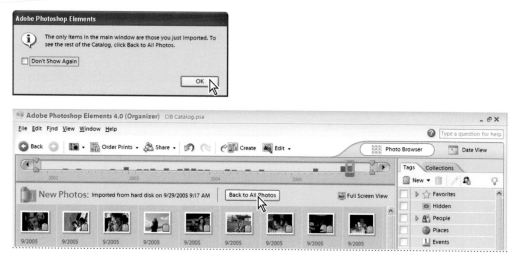

Reconnecting missing files to a catalog

After images are added to a catalog, Adobe Photoshop Elements expects them to remain in the same location. If you move the Lessons folder or any of the files after you have created the catalog, you may need to reconnect the files. This procedure is only necessary if you move the Lesson files or other images after you have imported them into the catalog. Photoshop Elements alerts you that it cannot find an image file, you will need to follow the following procedure. If your lesson files have not been moved, or you have not received an alert message regarding missing files, you do not need to follow this procedure and can go on to the first lesson.

Moving or renaming a catalogued image file or folder can break the catalog connections. Fortunately, reconnecting them is easy. If you ever receive a message that individual files cannot be located, simply complete the following steps:

1   Choose File > Reconnect > All Missing Files. If a message appears, "There are no files to reconnect," click OK, and then skip the rest of this procedure. Your files do not need to be reconnected.

2   If a message appears, "Searching for missing files," click the Browse button. The Reconnect Missing Files dialog box opens.

3   In the Browse tab on the right side of the Reconnect Missing Files dialog box, navigate to and open the Lessons folder.

4   Continuing to work in the Browse tab, locate and click once to select the folder that has the same name as the folder listed underneath the image thumbnail. The folder name is listed on the left side of the Reconnect Missing Files dialog box, directly under the image thumbnail.

5   After you select the appropriate folder and the correct thumbnail picture appears in the right side of the dialog box, click the Reconnect button.

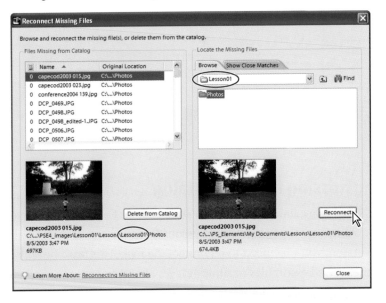

6   Repeat steps 4 and 5, continuing to select the appropriate folders, and clicking the Reconnect button as you find matching files. When all the files are reconnected, click the Close button.

You can now use the Photoshop Elements Organizer to select and open files in the Photoshop Elements Editor.

Note: This procedure also eliminates error messages regarding missing files when you work with Creations, or print from the Organizer.

Additional resources

Adobe Photoshop Elements 4.0 Classroom in a Book is not meant to replace documentation that comes with the program, nor is it designed to be a comprehensive reference for every feature in Photoshop Elements 4.0. For additional information about program features, refer to any of these resources:

• Photoshop Elements Help, which is built into the Adobe Photoshop Elements 4.0 application. You can view it by choosing Help > Photoshop Elements Help.

• The Adobe Web site (www.adobe.com), which you can view by choosing Help > Photoshop Elements Online. You can also choose Help > Online Support for access to the support pages on the Adobe Web site. Both of these options require that you have Internet access.

• The Adobe Photoshop Elements 4.0 Getting Started Guide, which is included either in the box with your copy of Adobe Photoshop Elements 4.0 or on the installation CD for the application software in PDF format. If you don't already have Adobe Reader (or if you have an older version of Adobe Acrobat Reader) installed on your computer, you can download a free copy from the Adobe Web site (www.adobe.com).

Adobe Certification

The Adobe Training and Certification Programs are designed to help Adobe customers improve and promote their product-proficiency skills. The Adobe Certified Expert (ACE) program is designed to recognize the high-level skills of expert users. Adobe Certified Training Providers (ACTP) use only Adobe Certified Experts to teach Adobe software classes. Available in either ACTP classrooms or on-site, the ACE program is the best way to master Adobe products. For Adobe Certified Training Programs information, visit the Partnering with Adobe Web site at http://partners.adobe.com.

1 | A Quick Tour of Photoshop Elements

This lesson introduces the tools and the interface of Adobe Photoshop Elements 4.0. Future lessons provide more in-depth exercises and specific details as to how you can take advantage of the tools.

This lesson provides the overview of the concepts and procedures involved with capturing and editing digital images using Photoshop Elements. If you prefer to skip this overview, you can jump right into working with digital images in Lesson 2. However, we encourage you to review this lesson before you get too far along in the book.

In this lesson, you'll learn how to do the following:

- Work with the Organizer and the Editor.
- Attach media.
- Use the Photo Downloader.
- Review and Compare Photos.
- Use Photo Compare.
- Make a greeting card from a template.
- Capture and export video.
- Use Help and the How To palette.

How Photoshop Elements works

Photoshop Elements has two primary workspaces: the Organizer for finding, organizing, and sharing photos and media files, and the Editor for creating, editing, and fixing your images.

When a photo is selected in the Organizer, clicking the Edit button and then choosing Go to Quick Fix or Go to Standard Edit moves the photo to the Editor workspace. When a photo is open in the Editor, clicking the Photo Browser or Date View button moves the photo to the Organizer workspace.

Use the buttons at the top of the work area to switch between the Organizer and the Editor.

💡 *Once both the Organizer and the Editor are open in Photoshop Elements, you can also move between the two workspaces by clicking the corresponding button in the Windows task bar at the bottom of the screen.*

The Organizer workspace

The Organizer lets you find, organize, and share your photos and media files in the Photo Browser. It can display a single photo or media file, or display thumbnails of all the photos and media files in your catalog. If you prefer viewing your photos and media files by date, the Organizer has a Date View workspace that lets you work with your files in a calendar format.

The Photo Browser lists all the photos and cataloged assets in one comprehensive window that you can easily browse through and filter. It can show previews of files stored remotely, such as files stored on a CD.

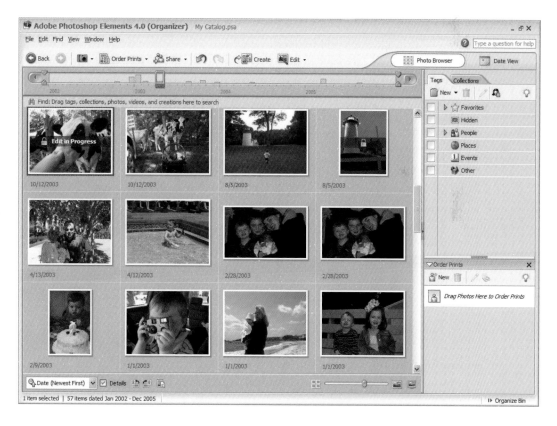

The Editor workspace

The Editor lets you focus on creating and editing images. The Standard Edit workspace has tools to correct color, create special effects, or enhance photos. There is also a Quick Fix workspace with simple tools and commands to quickly fix common problems.

If you are new to digital imaging, Quick Fix is a good place to start fixing photos. It has many basic tools for correcting color and lighting. See Lesson 4, "Adjusting Color in Images" for more detailed information.

If you've previously worked with image editing software, you'll find that the Standard Edit workspace provides a more flexible and powerful image-editing environment. It has lighting and color-correction commands, tools to fix image imperfections, selection tools, text editing tools, and painting tools. You can arrange the Standard Edit workspace to best suit your needs by moving, hiding, and showing palettes, arranging palettes in the Palette Bin, zooming in or out of the photo, scrolling to a different area of the document window, and creating multiple windows and views.

The Standard Edit workspace.

Workflow

The fundamental workflow for Adobe Photoshop Elements is to:

• Capture images and media into the Organizer from a digital camera, scanner, or digital video camera.

• Organize images and media using the Organizer, including tagging images.

• Edit images and media by color correcting or adding text, using the Editor.

• Sharing images and media by e-mailing, using a sharing service, or burning to CD/DVD ROM.

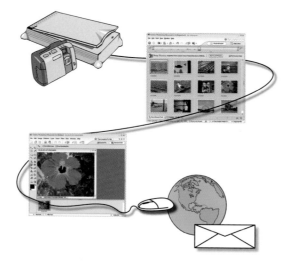

Attaching media

It's easy to import digital files directly into Photoshop Elements.

Getting photos from cameras, card readers, and from files and folders

To view and organize your photos in Photoshop Elements 4.0, you first need to bring them into the program. You can get photos into Photoshop Elements in several ways:

• Bring photos from your camera or card reader directly into the Photoshop Elements Organizer using Adobe Photo Downloader. Getting photos directly will save you time and allow you to start working with your photos quickly.

• Use the software that came with your digital camera to download pictures to your computer, and then bring them into Photoshop Elements using the From Files and Folders command. If you prefer to work with other software to import your files to your computer, you'll need to disable Adobe Photo Downloader to use the software that came with your camera. To disable the Adobe Photo Downloader, right-click the Adobe Photo Downloader icon in the system tray or task bar and then choose Disable. Only do this if you plan to use other software to bring images onto your computer.

• If your camera or card reader displays as a drive, e.g., in My Computer (Windows), you can drag the files to a folder on your hard drive, and then bring them into Photoshop Elements using the From Files and Folders command.

In most cases, you'll need to install software drivers that came with your camera before you can download pictures to your computer. You may also need to set up the Photoshop Elements Camera or Card Reader Preferences. See "Getting photos" in Lesson 2, "Organizing and Sharing Photos."

Creating a new catalog

You organize your photographs in catalogs, which manage the image files on your computer but are independent of the photo files themselves. You can include video and audio files along with digital photographs and scans in your catalogs. A single catalog can efficiently handle thousands of photos, but you can also create separate catalogs for different types of work to keep files independently.

1   Start Photoshop Elements, either by double-clicking the shortcut on your desktop or by choosing Start > Programs > Adobe Photoshop Elements 4.0.

2   Do one of the following:

• If the Welcome Screen appears, click View and Organize Photos in the row of shortcut buttons across the upper part of the Welcome window.

• If Photoshop Elements 4.0 (Editor) opens instead of the Welcome Screen, click the Photo Browser button (⊞) in the middle of the shortcuts bar across the upper part of the window. It takes about 10 seconds for the Organizer component to load for the first time in a work session.

• When Photoshop Elements 4.0 (Organizer) opens, you don't have to do anything more.

3   In Organizer mode, choose File > Catalog.

4   In the Catalog dialog box, click New.

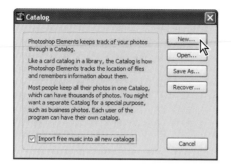

5   In the New Catalog dialog box, type **Lesson1** for File Name, and click Save without making any other changes to the settings.

Now you have a special catalog that you'll use just for this lesson. All you need is some pictures to put in it.

Using the Adobe Photo Downloader

For the rest of this lesson you will need to import images into the organizer. If you have a digital camera and images of your own, follow the steps in the next section. Otherwise, skip to the section, "To get photos from files and folders."

To get photos from a digital camera or card reader

You can import files from your camera directly into Photoshop Elements.

1   Connect your camera or card reader to your computer. For instructions on connecting your device, see the documentation that came with it.

2   When the Adobe Photo Downloader appears, choose the name of the connected camera or card reader from the Get Photos from drop-down menu.

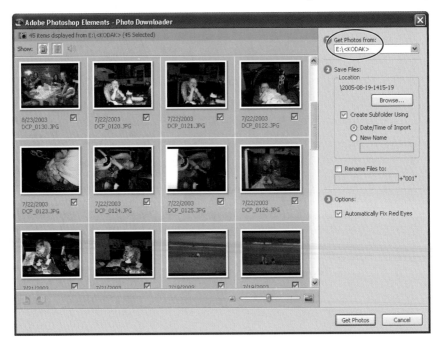

The connected device's name typically appears, as Photoshop Elements automatically detects your camera.

3 If the Windows Auto Play dialog box appears, click Cancel. If the Adobe Photo Downloader does not appear, click the Get Photos button in the shortcuts bar and then choose From Camera.

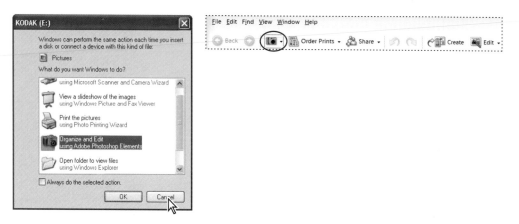

Thumbnail images of the photos in your camera's memory card appear.

4 Click the check box (removing the green check mark), to remove photos from the import list. Unchecked images are not imported.

You can drag the slider left or right to change the size of the thumbnails. You can also rotate any photo you bring in from a digital camera.

5 Select one or more photos to rotate. Click the Rotate Left button or the Rotate Right button located in the lower left of the Photo Downloader window.

6 Under Save Files, accept the folder location listed, or click Browse to choose a new location for the files.

7 Choose "Create Subfolder Using Date/Time of Import" if you want the photos you're getting to be stored in a folder whose name includes the date and time they were imported. You can also choose Create Subfolder Using > New Name to create a folder using a name you type in the text box.

8 Select "Rename Files to" and enter a file name in the text box to set the name for the imported photos. Each photo in the import batch will share the name, but each photo has a unique number after the name.

9 Click the Get Photos button.

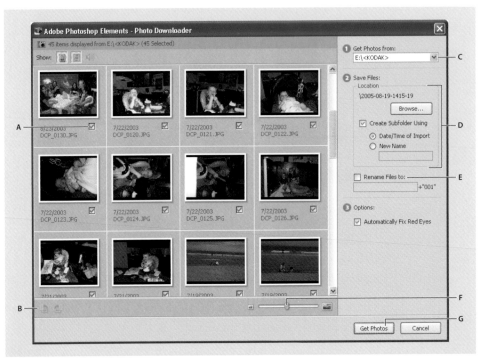

*A. Click box to download photo. **B**. Rotate buttons. **C**. Name of connected device. **D**. Options for saving files. **E**. Name for all files. **F**. Resize thumbnails in display. **G**. Gets the photos.*

The photos are imported into Photoshop Elements and appear in the Photo Browser.

After your photos are imported, you'll be asked if you'd like to delete those photos from the camera or card reader. Photos that you didn't bring into Photoshop Elements aren't deleted.

If the imported photos contain keyword metadata, the Import Attached Tags dialog box appears. Select the tags you want to import. The tags you select are added to the Tags palette when the photos are imported. If a tag has an asterisk (*), you already have a tag of the same name in your catalog, and that existing tag is attached to the photos.

To get photos from files and folders

Digital images stored on your computer can also be imported into Photoshop Elements.

1 In the Organizer, click the Get Photos button in the shortcuts bar, or choose Get Photos from the File menu and then choose From Files and Folders from the available choices.

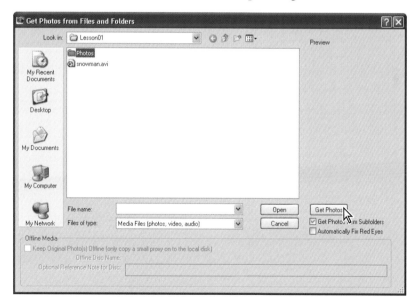

2 In the Get Photos dialog box, navigate to the Lesson01 folder and click once to select the Photos folder that contains sample images.

3 Click to uncheck the Automatically Fix Red Eyes checkbox. The photos being imported do not need red eye correction.

4 Click Get Photos. These images contain tags, which you'll learn more about in Lesson 2. In the Import Attached Tags window, click Select All, then click OK. The imported photos appear in the Organizer.

About tags

Tags are personalized keywords, such as "House" or "Beach," that you attach to photos, video clips, audio clips, and creations in the Photo Browser to easily organize and find them. When you use tags, there's no need to manually organize your photos in subject-specific folders or rename files with content-specific names. Instead, you simply attach one or more tags to each photo. You can then easily retrieve the photos you want by clicking the appropriate tags in the Tags palette.

For example, you can create a tag called "Doreen" and attach it to every photo featuring your sister, Doreen. You can then instantly find all the photos with the Doreen tag by clicking the Find box next to the Doreen tag in the Tags palette, regardless of where the photos are stored on your computer.

You can create tags using any keywords you want. For instance, you can create tags for individual people, places, and events in your life. You can attach multiple tags to your photos. When photos have multiple tags, you can easily search on a combination of tags to find a particular person at a particular place or event. For example, you can search for all "Doreen" tags and all "Scott" tags to find all pictures of Doreen with her husband, Scott. Or search for all "Doreen" tags and all "Florida" tags to find all the pictures of Doreen vacationing in Florida.

Use tags to organize and find photos by their content. You specify names for your tags and choose the photos that fall into those categories. See Lesson 2, "Organizing and Sharing Photos" for more information.

Reviewing and comparing

Photoshop Elements provides several options to quickly and easily review and compare images.

Viewing photos at full screen or side-by-side

The Full Screen View and Side by Side View let you review your images without the distraction of other interface items such as windows, menus, and palettes.

In the Organizer, choose View > View Photos in Full Screen. Your photos are displayed as a full-screen slide show, making it a fun and efficient way to view a set of photos. You can customize the slide show—for example, you can play an audio file as you view the images. You can also choose to display thumbnails of the selected files in a filmstrip along the right side of the screen, or add a fade between pictures. Click OK to start the Slide Show.

The control bar, which contains buttons for playing, rotating, and zooming disappears from view when you don't move the mouse for a couple seconds. To make the control bar reappear, move the mouse.

When you've decided which photos you want in your slide show, and you've made necessary edits to them, you can send them directly from this view to the Slide Show Editor by clicking the Create Slide Show button in the control bar. You'll work on one complete Slide Show project in Lesson 3, "Sharing Creations."

Press the Esc key on your keyboard to return to the Organizer.

Choose View > Compare Photos Side by Side to display two photos simultaneously. Side by Side view is useful when you need to focus on details and differences between photos. You can select two or more photos to compare. When you click the Next Photo button (⏯) in the control bar, the selected image changes to the next image in your catalog. By default, image # 1 (on the left or top) is selected. To select image #2 instead, click it.

Note: *The selected image has a blue border. If you have the filmstrip showing, you can click on any image in the filmstrip to view it in place of the selected image.*

Use Side by Side View to analyze composition and details.

You can switch between views by clicking the Full Screen View button (▢) or the Side by Side View button (▢▢) in the control bar. While in either view, you can mark your favorites for printing, fix red eye, add a photo to a collection, zoom in, rotate, delete, and apply tags to a photo. Press the Esc key to return to the Organizer.

Choosing files

To select more than one photo in the Photo Browser, hold down the Ctrl key and click the photos you want to select. Holding down the Ctrl key allows you to select multiple, non-consecutive files. To select photos that are in a consecutive order, hold down the Shift key and click the first photo, then click the last photo you want. All the photos between the selected photos will be selected as well.

Choose the photos to be compared in the Organizer by holding the Ctrl key and selecting the images. Then choose View > Compare Photos Side by Side.

Making a greeting card

You can use a variety of templates to create cards that you can print on your home printer and then mail to others.

1   In the Photo Browser, select the photo you'd like to use for a postcard.

2   Click the Create button (🖼) in the shortcuts bar to show the Creation Setup window.

3   Select Photo Greeting Card from the list of creation types, and then click OK.

4   Select a style from the list on the right, and then click Next Step.

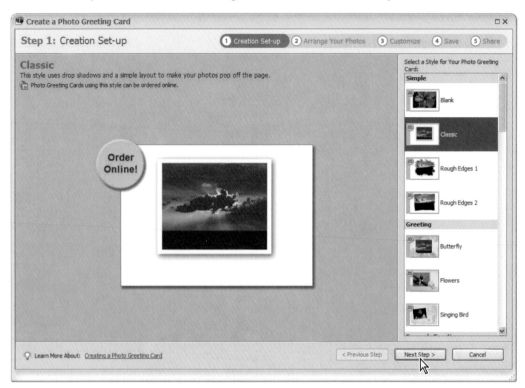

5   To use the displayed photo, click Next Step. To select a different picture, click Add Photos in the upper left corner, select a new photo, and then click Next Step.

6   Reposition or resize the photo as needed.

7   Double-click the sample text to customize it with your specific text. Use the Title dialog box to enter text and choose formatting options, then click Done.

8   Click Next Step.

9 Type a name for your card in the Photo Greeting Card Name text box, or select Use Title for Name.

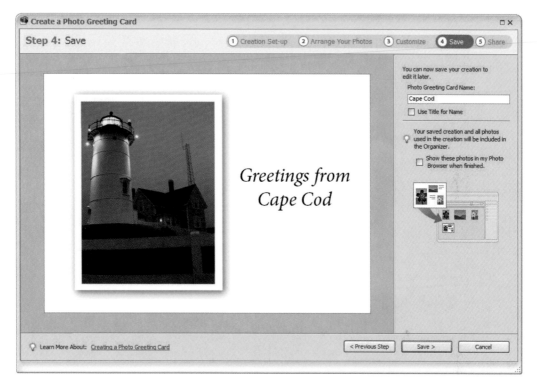

10 Click Save.

11 Choose how you'd like to share your card. You can create a PDF, print it on your home printer, e-mail the photo greeting card, or order it online. When you're finished, click Done to close the Creations Wizard.

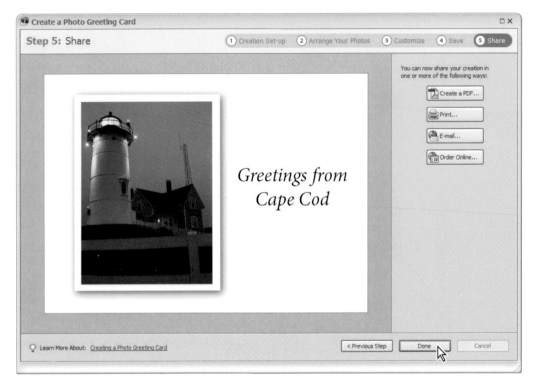

Video format support

If you record digital video from a camcorder, Photoshop Elements can import frames and manage them as graphic files.

To acquire still frames from a video

You can capture frames from your digital videos if they are saved in a file format that Photoshop Elements can open, including AVI, MPG, MPEG, WMV, ASF, and MLV. To capture frames from video, you'll need to open the Editor.

1 Choose Edit > Deselect to deselect the card that was added to the Catalog in the previous exercise.

2   Select Edit > Go to Standard Edit in the shortcuts bar to open the Editor.

3   In the Editor, choose File > Import > Frame from Video.

4   In the Frame from Video dialog box, click the Browse button, navigate to the Lesson01 folder and choose snowman.avi, then click Open.

5   To start the video, click the Play button (▶).

6   To get a frame of the video as a still image, click the Grab Frame button or press the spacebar when the frame is visible on the screen. You can move forward and backward in the video to capture additional frames.

Note: Some video formats don't support rewinding or fast-forwarding. In these cases, the Rewind (◀◀) and Fast Forward (▶▶) buttons are dimmed.

7   When you have all the frames you want, click Done.

8   Save the still files in Photoshop Elements.

Using Help

The complete documentation for using Adobe Photoshop Elements is available by using Help.

Note: Adobe Help systems include all the information in the printed user guides, plus additional information.

To navigate Help

Choose Help > Photoshop Elements Help... to open the Help Center. Click Product Help, and do any of the following:

• To view Photoshop Elements Help, choose Adobe Photoshop Elements 4.0 from the Help For menu.

• To expand or collapse a section, click the blue triangle to the left of the section name.

• To display a topic, click its title.

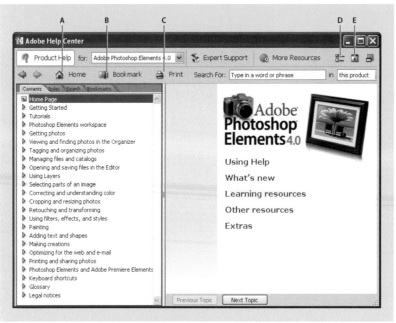

*A. Returns you to Help home page. **B**. Adds bookmark for current topic.*
*C. Prints contents of right pane. **D**. Opens Preferences dialog box.*
E. Opens About Adobe Help Center window.

To search Help topics

Search Help using words or phrases to quickly find topics. You can search Help for only Photoshop Elements or for all Adobe products you've installed. If you find a topic that you may want to view again, you can bookmark it for quick retrieval.

1   In Adobe Help Center, click Product Help. Type one or more words in the Search box. To search across Help for all Adobe products you have installed, click the black triangle to the left of the Search box and choose Search All Help.

2   Click Search. Topics matching the search words appear in the navigation pane.

3   To view a topic, click its title in the navigation pane.

4   To return to the navigation pane, do one of the following:

• Click the Home button (🏠).

• Click the Back button (◀).

• Click the Next Topic button or Previous Topic button at the bottom.

5   Close the Help window.

Search tips

Adobe Help Search works by searching the entire Help text for topics that contain all the words typed in the Search box. These tips can help you improve your search results in Help:

• If you search using a phrase, such as "shape tool," put quotation marks around the phrase. The search returns only those topics containing all words in the phrase.

• Make sure that the search terms are spelled correctly.

• If a search term doesn't yield results, try using a synonym, such as "photo" instead of "picture."

To use the How To palette

In the Standard Edit workspace, the How To palette provides activities that guide you through different image-editing tasks. For example, you can view instructions about restoring an old photograph. Photoshop Elements will even perform some of the steps for you.

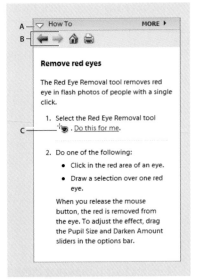

How To palette.
A. Click the triangle to open or close the palette.
B. Navigation and Print buttons.
C. Click Do this for me to have Photoshop
Elements perform the task.

1   Open the How To palette by clicking its triangle in the Palette Bin or by choosing Window > How To.

2   Choose a category and click the How To topic you want to use.

Note: *You can use the navigation arrows to move between the How To topics. The Home button takes you back to the main menu.*

3   Follow the How To instructions. When available, you can click Do this for me to have Photoshop Elements perform the task for you. If you want to print a set of instructions, click the Print button (🖶).

Hot-linked tips

Hot-linked tips are available throughout Adobe Photoshop Elements 4. These tips display information in the form of a typical tip balloon, or they will link you to the appropriate topic in the help file.

You've reached the end of the first lesson. Now that you understand how to get photos and the essentials of the Photoshop Elements interface you are ready to start organizing and editing photos—which you'll do in the next lesson.

Review

> ## Review questions

1 What are the primary workspaces in Adobe Photoshop Elements 4.0?

2 Define the fundamental workflow of Adobe Photoshop Elements 4.0.

3 What are tags?

4 What digital video formats are supported by Adobe Photoshop Elements 4.0?

> ## Review answers

1 Photoshop Elements has two main workspaces: the Organizer workspace for finding, organizing, and sharing photos and media files, and the Editor workspace for creating, editing, and fixing your images.

2 The fundamental workflow in Adobe Photoshop Elements involves:

    a Capturing media into the Organizer from a digital camera, scanner, digital video camera, or image created from scratch in the editing component.

    b Categorize the media in the Organizer using the tag assignment features.

    c Edit the media by color correcting or adding text, using the Editor.

    d Share the media by e-mailing, using a sharing service or burning to CD/DVD ROM.

3 Tags are personalized keywords such as "House" or "Beach" that you attach to photos, video clips, audio clips, and creations in the Photo Browser so that you can easily organize and find them.

4 The digital video formats that are supported by Adobe Photoshop Elements 4.0 include: AVI, MPG, MPEG, WMV, ASF, and MLV.

2 Organizing and Sharing Photos

After capturing your memories with your digital camera, you'll want to keep track of your pictures and share them with others. This lesson gets you started with the essential skills you'll need to track and share your images.

In this lesson you will learn how to do the following:

- Open Adobe Photoshop Elements 4.0 in Organizer mode.

- Create a catalog of your images.

- Import images from a digital camera or scanner onto your computer and into a catalog.

- Apply automatic fixes to photos to correct common problems.

- Crop a photo to include only the part of the picture you want.

- Change the display of thumbnails in your catalog.

- Create, organize, and apply tags to images.

Photoshop Elements 4.0 for Windows includes two primary parts: the Editor and the Organizer. Together they work hand-in-hand to help you find, share, and make corrections to your photographs and images.

Before you start working in Adobe Photoshop Elements 4.0, make sure that you have installed the software on your computer from the application CD. (See "Installing Adobe Photoshop Elements 4.0" on page 3.)

Also make sure that you have correctly copied the Lessons folder from the CD in the back of this book onto your computer hard disk. (See "Copying the Classroom in a Book files" on page 3.)

Most people need between one and two hours to complete all the projects in this lesson.

Getting started

In this lesson, you're going to work primarily in the Organizer component of Photoshop Elements.

1 Start Photoshop Elements, either by double-clicking the shortcut on your desktop or by choosing Start > Programs > Adobe Photoshop Elements 4.0.

2 Do one of the following:

• If the Welcome Screen appears, click View and Organize Photos in the row of shortcut buttons across the upper part of the Welcome window.

• If Photoshop Elements 4.0 (Editor) opens instead of the Welcome Screen, click the Photo Browser button (🖉⊞) in the middle of the shortcuts bar across the upper part of the window. It takes about 10 seconds for the Organizer component to load for the first time in a work session.

• If Photoshop Elements 4.0 (Organizer) opens, you don't have to do anything more.

Getting photos

The Organizer component of Photoshop Elements gives you a gathering place where you can efficiently organize, sort, and perform basic editing of your pictures. When you want to print your photographs or send them with an e-mail, having the images collected in the Organizer is an essential step in the process, as you'll see later in this lesson.

Creating a new catalog

Photoshop Elements organizes your photographs in catalogs, which manage the image files on your computer. Catalogs are independent of the photo files themselves. You can include video and audio files along with digital photographs and scans in your catalogs. A single catalog can efficiently handle thousands of photos, but you can also create separate catalogs for different types of work. You'll create a new catalog now so that you won't confuse the practice files for this lesson with the other lesson files for this book.

1 In Photoshop Elements 4.0 (Organizer), choose File > Catalog.

Note: In this book, the forward arrow character (>) is used to refer to commands and submenus found in the menus at the top of the application window, for example, File, Edit, and so forth.

2   In the Catalog window, click New.

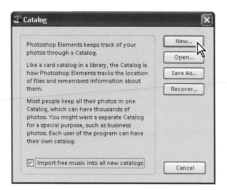

3   In the New Catalog window, type **Lesson2** for File name, and click Save without making any other changes to the settings.

You will use this catalog to import the images for this lesson.

Dragging photos from Windows Explorer

This method of adding photographs to an Organizer catalog couldn't be easier or more intuitive. It uses the familiar drag-and-drop technique.

1   Minimize the Organizer by clicking the Minimize button (▬) on the right side of the title bar. Or, click the application button on the Windows taskbar to minimize it.

2   Open My Computer by whatever method you usually use, such as double-clicking an icon on the desktop, using the Start menu, or using Windows Explorer.

Note: If you need help finding Windows Explorer or navigating the multi-leveled folder structure on your computer, see Windows Help (click Start and choose Help and Support).

3   Resize and arrange the My Computer window so that it does not fill the screen. Then reopen the Organizer and resize it, as needed, so that you can see both windows.

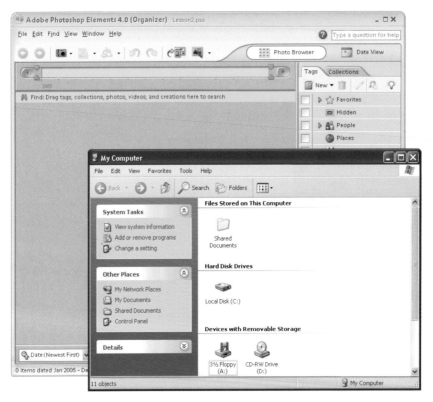

4   In My Computer, navigate through the folder structure on your computer to find and open the Lessons folder that you copied, and then select and open the Lesson02 folder. If you don't see the Lessons folder, see "Copying the Classroom in a Book files" on page 3.

You'll see three folders inside the Lesson02 folder: BATCH1, BATCH2, and BATCH3.

5   Drag the BATCH1 folder into the Organizer. These files have tags applied to them to help keep them organized, so the Import Attached Tags dialog box opens. Click Select All, then click OK.

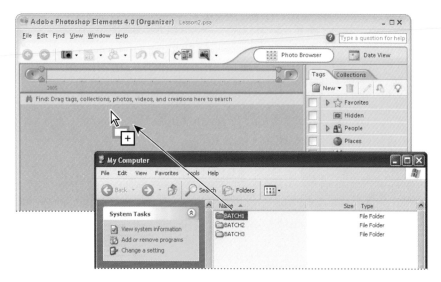

6   If a message appears, telling you that only the newly imported files will appear, click OK.

7   Click the Maximize button in the upper right corner of the Organizer window. This causes the window to expand and cover the entire screen.

You can now see thumbnails of the four images you've added to your Lesson2 catalog. Don't drag the other two batches into the Organizer, because you're going to use different methods of adding them to your catalog.

Getting photos from specific locations

A second technique for adding photographs to your catalog is similar to the first one, but you use a menu command instead of having to resize and arrange windows on the desktop.

1   Choose File > Get Photos > From Files and Folders.

2   In the Get Photos from Files and Folders dialog box, navigate to the Lessons\ Lesson02 folder, and open the BATCH2 folder.

3   One by one, select each of the four image files in the BATCH2 folder, and look at the Preview area to see a thumbnail of each image.

While none of these images need red eye correction, you can quickly remove red eye automatically while importing images into the Photo Browser. To remove red eye automatically, check the checkbox Automatically Fix Red Eyes in the Get Photos from Files and Folders dialog box. Additional ways to fix red eye will be discussed later in this lesson.

4   Select 02_05.jpg. Then hold down Shift and select 02_08.jpg to select the four images.

5   Click the Get Photos button.

6   Click OK to close any other alert window. In the Import Attached Tags dialog box, click Select All, then click OK.

7   Click the Back to All Photos button above the thumbnails area to see all eight images.

Now you have a total of eight images in your Lesson2 catalog. The thumbnails are arranged according to the date each image file was created.

💡 *You can also click the camera icon below the menu bar to access the Get Photos options.*

Searching for photos to add

This method is probably the one you'll want to use if you're not sure where in your folder structure you've stashed photographs and other resources over the years. Ordinarily, you might run this search on your entire hard disk or for the entire My Documents folder. For this demonstration, you'll limit your search area to a very restricted part of the folder organization on your computer.

1   In the Organizer, choose File > Get Photos > By Searching.

2   In the dialog box that appears, choose Browse from the Look In drop-down menu.

3 In the Browse For Folder window, click to select the Lesson02 folder, and then click OK.

4 Click the Search button.

5 In the Search Results, click to select only the BATCH3 folder, and then click the Import Folders button. In the Import Attached Tags window, click Select All, then click OK.

6 In the Organizer, examine the newly imported image thumbnails, and then click Back to All Photos.

Importing from a digital camera

This exercise is optional and requires that you have an available digital camera or memory card from your camera with pictures on it. You can either do this procedure now or skip to the Viewing photo thumbnails section later in this lesson.

1   Connect your digital camera or the card reader for your digital camera to your computer, following the manufacturer's instructions for your camera.

2   Do one of the following:

•   If the Get Photos from Camera or Card Reader window appears automatically, wait while Photoshop Elements collects information from your camera.

•   If a different window appears, click Cancel. Then, in the Organizer, choose File > Get Photos > From Camera or Card Reader. When the Photo Downloader window appears, select your camera or card reader in the Get Photos from drop-down menu.

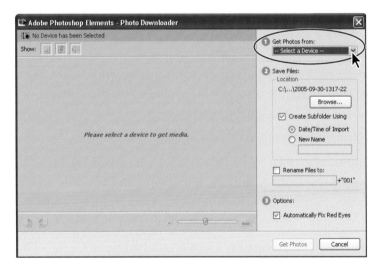

3   When the downloader finishes collecting thumbnails from the camera or memory card, scroll down the left side of the window to see the thumbnails.

4   Click the check boxes to deselect any images you don't want to download.

5 Drag the slider in the lower right corner of the thumbnails area to reduce or enlarge the size of the thumbnails. Or, click the icons at either end of the slider to jump to maximum or minimum thumbnail size.

6 (Optional) On the right side of the Get Photos from Camera or Card Reader dialog box, under (2) Save Files, select the options you want for storing the images:

• Create Subfolder Using option stores the downloaded images in a separate folder within the Digital Camera Photos folder.

• Date/Time of Import names the folder based on the current date and time. For example, 2005-08-24-16-13-26 for August 24, 2005 at 4:13:26 PM), or select New Name and type a name in the space provided to customize the name of the folder.

• Click Browse to customize where the images will be stored. If you prefer a different location (the default is My Documents\My Pictures\Adobe\Digital Camera Photos), select it in the Browse for Folder dialog box, and click OK.

7 (Optional) Select Rename Files to, and type an appropriate prefix for the file name. For example, type **2005 Vacation** to name the images 2005 Vacation001, 2005 Vacation002, 2005 Vacation003, and so forth.

8 Click Get Photos.

Photoshop Elements will go to work, downloading the images from the camera or memory card. When it finishes, the pictures will appear in the Organizer and are copied to your computer's hard drive.

Importing from a scanner

This exercise is also optional and requires that you have an available scanner.

1 Turn on your scanner, if it is not already on, and place the picture or document you want to scan in the scanner bed.

2 If the Get Photos from Scanner dialog box does not appear automatically, go to the Organizer and choose File > Get Photos > From Scanner.

3 In the dialog box, do the following:

• Make sure that the correct scanner is selected in the Scanner drop-down menu, if you have more than one scanner installed.

• If you want to change the location in which the scanned files will be saved, choose Browse. Then find and select the folder you want to use.

• Either leave the default Save As settings unchanged (jpeg), and Quality (6 Medium), or if you want different settings, change them now.

4 Click OK.

5 In the scan window, click the Preview button, and examine the resulting image.

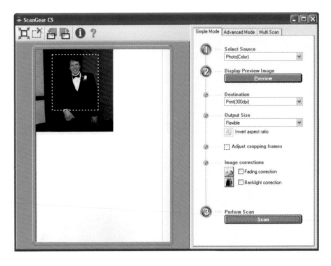

Note: The general appearance of the dialog box and the options available for your scanner may vary from those shown in the illustrations.

6 (Optional) If you want to make adjustments, click Advanced Mode, and change the settings as needed.

7 Click Scan.

When the scan is complete, the image thumbnail appears in the Organizer.

8   Click Back to All Images to see your entire catalog.

💡 *When you scan several photographs together, Photoshop Elements can automatically crop the scan into individual photos and straighten them. For more information on the Divide Scanned Photos feature, see Photoshop Elements Help.*

Using watched folders

Watched folders are folders on your computer that automatically alert Photoshop Elements when a new photo is saved or added to the folder. By default, the My Pictures folder is watched, but you can add additional folders to the list. New images added to these folders can be automatically added to the Organizer.

You can set up watched folders in two ways. You can choose to have new photos detected in a watched folder automatically added to your catalog, or you can opt to be asked before photos are added. When you choose this option, the message "New files have been found in Watched Folders" appears when photos are added. Just click Yes to add the photos to your catalog, or click No to skip them.

Now you'll add a folder to the watched folders list.

1   Choose File > Watch Folders.

2   Click Add, and then browse to the Lesson02 folder.

3   Select the Lesson02 folder and then click OK. The folder name appears in the Folders to Watch list. Keep the Notify Me option selected, then click OK to close the Watch Folders window.

Viewing photo thumbnails in the Organizer

There are several ways to view your Organizer catalog. While some display preferences let you change the display to meet your needs, other options can make it easier to work with items in the Organizer.

Using Photo Browser view

Up to this point, you've been working in the default Photo Browser view. The Organizer also has other options for displaying images.

1   In the drop-down menu in the lower left corner of the Organizer window, select Import Batch to see the thumbnails organized by their separate import sessions. Notice the bar and film canister icons (📷) separating the each row of thumbnails from each other.

2 Try the following:

• Click the separator bar between two batches (reading "Imported from hard disk on...") to select the thumbnails of all images imported in that session.

• Enlarge the thumbnail size by dragging the slider below the thumbnail area.

• Click one of the three bars in the graph above the thumbnails area to jump to the first image imported in that session.

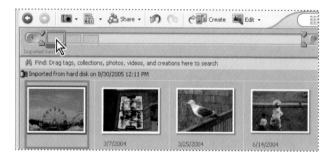

The view switches to the first image in that batch, the date for that image flashes off and on, and a green border temporarily surrounds the image.

3 Reduce the thumbnail size again before you continue, making it small enough so that you can see all the images in your catalog.

4   Using the same drop-down menu that you used in Step 1, select Folder Location to see the thumbnails organized according to the folders in which they are stored on your computer.

5   Repeat the same steps you performed in Step 2.

6   Using the same drop-down menu, select Date (Newest First). Select one of the bars in the graph above the thumbnails to jump to the photographs taken at the selected point in the timeline.

Note: To display the file name of individual images in the Organizer, choose Edit > Preferences > General. In the Preferences window, select Show File Names in Details.

Using Date View

If you are working with a collection of pictures that span a number of years, Date View is a great way to organize your images.

1 Select Date View (⊞) on the right end of the shortcuts bar.

2 Select the Year option under the calendar display (bottom center left), if it is not already selected. Use the right and left arrows on either side of the year heading in the calendar to go to 2004, if it is not already selected.

3 Select March 25 on the 2004 calendar.

A preview of the photograph taken on March 25 appears on the right.

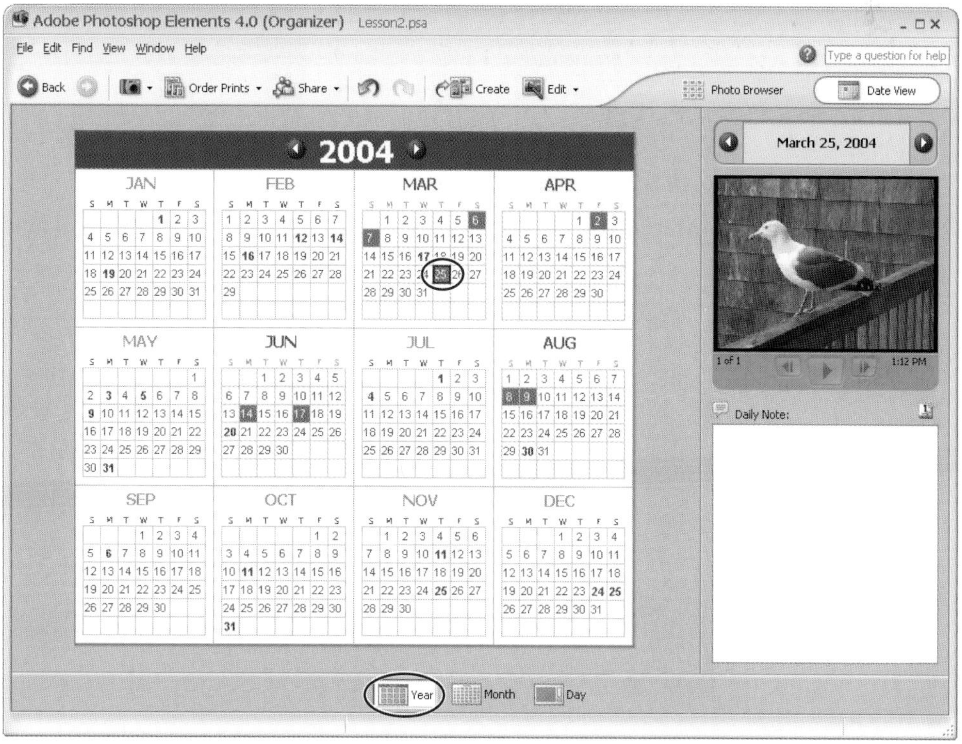

4 Select the Month option under the calendar display, and then select March 6 on the calendar, where there's already a thumbnail of a flower photograph.

5 Under the flower thumbnail on the right, click the Next Item On Selected Day arrow to see another photograph taken on the same date.

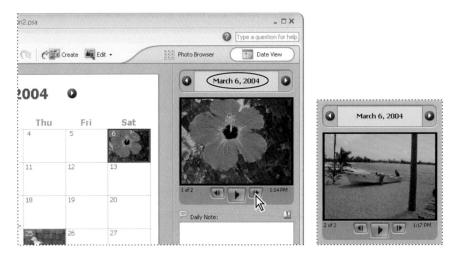

6 Using the date at the top of the calendar, do the following:

• Click the word March and choose August from the menu of months that appears.

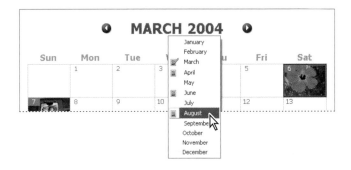

• Click 2004 in the calendar heading and choose 2003 from the menu of years.

7 Click in the Daily Note area (bottom right) and type **County Fair** to add a note to the date.

Now that you know how to change the date to review your images, you can reset the Organizer to your preferred settings whenever you want to do so. For these lessons, you'll go back to Photo Browser rather than Date View.

Organizing photos

Most of us find it challenging to organize our files and folders efficiently. It's easy to forget which pictures were stored in what folder. It's tedious to have to open and examine the contents of numerous folders, looking for images or files.

The good news is that such searches are a thing of the past. You saw earlier how you can use the Search feature in the Organizer to find and import files from multiple locations on your computer. The next set of topics will show you how a little time invested in tags can streamline the process of sorting through your pictures, regardless of where the image files are stored.

About stacks

You can create stacks to visually group a set of similar photos together, making them easy to manage. Stacks are useful for keeping multiple photos of the same subject in one place, and they reduce clutter in the Photo Browser.

For instance, you can create a stack to group together multiple photos of your family taken with the same pose, or for photos taken at a sports event using your camera's burst mode or auto-bracket feature. Generally, when you take photos this way, you end up with many variations of the same photo, but you only want the best one to appear in the Photo Browser. Stacking the photos lets you easily access them all in one place instead of having them scattered across rows of thumbnails.

You'll create a stack now.

1   Choose the Photo Browser button, located at the top right side of the screen, to view the Lesson 2 catalog thumbnails.

2   Select Import Batch from the drop-down menu in the bottom left corner of the Photo Browser window.

3   Select the photos in the top row, which is the first batch of photos imported. To select multiple images, click to select the first image, then press the Shift key and click the last image in the row. All images in the row become selected.

4 Choose Edit > Stack > Stack Selected Photos to create a group of stacked photos. The selected images are placed into a stack.

5 Choose Edit > Stack > Reveal Photos in Stack to display all images in the stack.

6 Click the Back to All Photos button.

7 Choose Edit > Stack > Unstack Photos. The photos are no longer displayed in a stack.

Tips for working with stacks

Keep these points in mind when working with stacks:

• By default, the newest photo is placed on top of the stack. As you create the stack, you can specify a new top photo by right-clicking the photo you want on top and using the context menus.

• Combining two or more stacks merges them to form one new stack. The original stacks are not preserved. The newest photo is placed on top of the stack.

- Many actions applied to a stack, such as editing, e-mailing, and printing, are applied to the topmost item only. To apply an action to all photos in a stack, reveal the stacked photos or unstack the photos.

- If you apply a tag to a collapsed stack, the tag is applied to all items in the stack. When you run a search on the tag, the top photo with the tag icon appears in the search results. If you want to apply a tag to only one photo in a stack, reveal that photo in the stack and then apply the tag.

- You can access stack commands by right-clicking or by using the Edit menu.

About Picture Package

Picture Package lets you place multiple copies of one or more photos on a single printed page. You can choose from a variety of size and placement options to customize your package layout.

You'll select one of the pictures in the Lesson2 catalog to create a picture package.

1   Select any picture from the browser and choose File > Print.

2   In the Print Selected Photos dialog box, choose a printer from the Select Printer menu.

3   Choose Picture Package from the Select Type of Print menu. If a Printing Warning window appears, click OK. The Printing Warning cautions against enlarging the pictures. You will print multiple smaller pictures.

4   Choose Letter (4) 2.5 x 3.5 (8) 2 x 2.5 from the Select a Layout menu, and click the Fill Page With First Photo checkbox.

Note: Depending on the layout you choose, the images are oriented to produce the optimum coverage of the printable area. This feature is automatic and cannot be overridden. You cannot rotate the images placed in the layout.

5   Choose Heart Felt or another border from the Select a Frame menu. You can select only one border for the picture package.

To print the images listed in the dialog box on separate pages, click the Fill Page with First Photo option. You can use the Navigation buttons below the layout preview to view each layout.

6 To crop photos so they fit the layout size perfectly, click Crop to Fit.

Note: If you want to add a photo to your picture package layout and it's not listed in the Print Photos dialog box, click the Add button and use the Add Photos dialog box to select the photos you want. Click Done to add the selected photos to the list in the Print Photos dialog box. To replace a photo in the layout, drag an image from the left side of the Print Photos dialog box over an image in the layout preview, and release the mouse button.

7 Click Print to print the package on your computer.

Working with version sets

A version set is a type of stack that contains one original photo and edited versions of the original. Version sets make it easy to find both the edited versions of an image and the original, because they are visually stacked together instead of scattered throughout the Photo Browser.

Now you'll use Auto Smart Fix to edit an image in the organizer and create a version set.

1 Select an image in the Organizer, such as the flower from BATCH1.

2 Choose Edit > Auto Smart Fix. The Organizer automatically puts the photo and its edited copy together in a version set.

Version sets are identified by a stack icon in the upper right corner of an image.

3 Click to select the version set in the Photo Browser view within the Organizer.

4   Choose Edit > Version Set > Reveal Items in Version Set to see the original and edited images.

Edit		
⟲ Undo Auto Smart Fix	Ctrl+Z	
⟳ Redo	Ctrl+Y	
📋 Copy	Ctrl+C	
Set as Desktop Wallpaper	Ctrl+Shift+W	
Stack	▸	
Version Set	▸	Reveal Items in Version Set
Color Settings...	Ctrl+Alt+G	Flatten Version Set...
👥 Contact Book...		Convert Version Set to Individual Items
Preferences	▸	⟲ Revert to Original...
		Remove Item(s) from Version Set
		Set as Top Item

5   Click the Back to All Photos button to view all photos in the catalog.

Note: When you edit the photo in Standard Edit or Quick Fix and choose File > Save As, you can select the Save in Version Set with Original option to put the photo and its edited copy together in a version set.

If you edit a photo that's already in a stack, the photo and its edited copy are put in a version set that is nested in the original stack. If you edit a photo that's already in a version set, the edited copy is placed at the top of the existing version set.

To remove red eye in the Photo Browser

Red eye is caused by a reflection of the subject's retina created by the camera's flash. You'll see it more often when taking pictures in a darkened room.

While Photoshop Elements can automatically fix red eyes when you bring photos into the Organizer, here you'll use another method for fixing red eye. Select Automatically Fix Red Eyes in the Get Photos from Files and Folders dialog box when you import your photos.

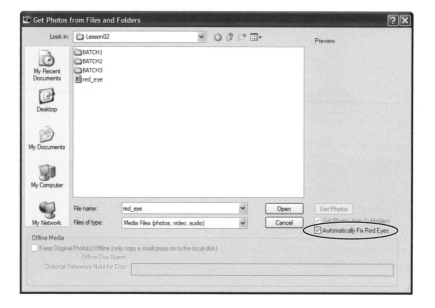

In addition, you can remove red eye from one or more selected photos while viewing them in the Photo Browser.

1   Choose > File > Get Photos > From Files and Folders…

2   Select the image red_eye from the Lesson02 folder.

3   If necessary, uncheck the Automatically Fix Red Eyes checkbox, and click Get Photos.

4   In the Import Attached Tags window, click Select All, then click OK. Click OK if you receive an alert that only the imported items are displayed.

5   Select the photo in the browser window, and choose > Edit > Auto Red Eye Fix.

A progress window will appear displaying the progress of the red eye fix. When the fix is complete, an Auto Fix Red Eye dialog box may appear informing you that a version set was created. Check Don't Show Again, and then click OK.

6   Choose Edit > Go to Standard Edit... to view the results in the editor.

7   Select the Zoom Tool (🔍) from the tool box and click three times between the two boys' heads to view the results of the Auto Fix Red Eye feature.

Note: If you prefer, you can use the Red Eye Removal tool. See "Working with red eye" in Lesson 4.

8   Choose File > Close to close the file and return to the Photo Browser.

Viewing and finding photos

In the Organizer, Photoshop Elements lets you find photos using several methods:

•   **Timeline**—Click a month or set a range to find photos and media files chronologically by date, import batch, or folder location.

•   **Find bar**—Drag and drop a photo, tag, creation, or collection onto the find bar to locate matching or similar photos and media files.

- **Find menu**—Use the commands in this menu to find photos by date, caption or note, file name, history, media type, metadata, or color similarity. Commands are also available for finding photos and media files that have unknown dates, are untagged, or are not in any collection.

Finding photos using details and metadata

You can search for your images by file details or metadata. Searching by metadata is useful when you want to search using multiple criteria at once. For example, if you want to find all photos captured on 2/3/05 that include the "Sister" tag, you can search using both capture date and tags in the Find by Details (Metadata) dialog box.

Searchable metadata includes criteria such as file name, file type, tags, collections, notes, author, capture date, as well as camera model, shutter speed, and F-stop.

Here you will search using a variety of photo details at one time using the Find by Details (Metadata) dialog box.

1   Choose Find > By Details (Metadata) in the Photo Browser to display the Find by Details (Metadata) dialog box.

2   Choose F-Stop for the first search criteria and Is between for the second. Then choose 1.00 and 2.80 for the F-stop values.

3   Click the Search button. All images that match the specified criteria are displayed.

4   Click the Back to All Photos button after reviewing the search result.

Note: *To include other metadata values in your search, click the plus (+) sign and specify new values using the menus that appear. To remove metadata from your search, click the minus (-) sign along the right side of the metadata you want to remove. To modify the search, click the Modify button in the find bar, make changes as desired, and then click OK.*

To view and manage files by their folder location

The Folder Location view in the Organizer splits the Photo Browser into three sections: a folder hierarchy panel on the left, an image thumbnail panel in the center, and the Palette Bin on the right. From this view you can manage your folders, add files to your catalog, automatically tag files using their folder name as the tag, and add or remove folders from Watched Folder status.

By default, the left panel displays all the folders on your hard disk, and the center panel displays only the thumbnails of the managed files in the selected folder. Folders containing managed files have a Managed folder icon (📁). Watched folders have a Watched folder icon (📁).

The contents of a selected folder are displayed when using Folder Location view.

Note: *You can change the default view for each panel by choosing Edit > Preferences > Folder Location View and selecting the options you want.*

1   Choose Folder Location from the Photo Browser Arrangement drop-down menu in the lower left corner of the window.

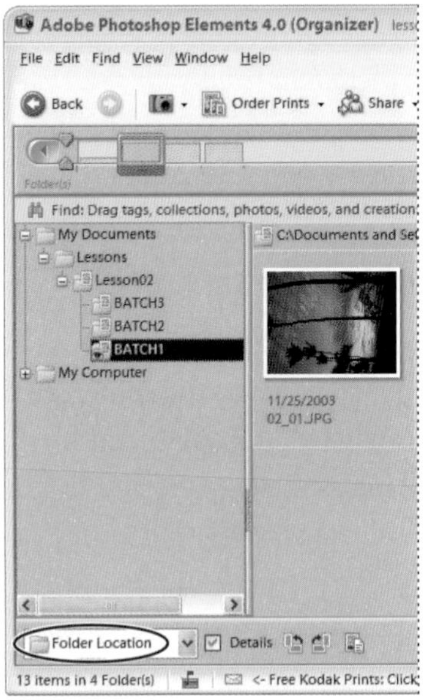

The folder hierarchy appears on the left side of the window and the image thumbnails appear in the center.

2   Do any of the following to specify which folders appear in the left panel:

•   To view only the folders that contain Photoshop Elements managed files, right-click in the left panel and, if necessary, deselect Show All Folders. This option is useful if you want to limit the number of folders displaying to just your watched folders and those containing managed images.

•   To view all the folders on your hard disk, right-click in the left panel and select Show All Folders. This option is useful if you want to add files from folders that don't currently include managed files.

3   Do one of the following to specify which files appear in the center panel:

•   To view only the managed files in the selected folder, right-click in the left panel and deselect Show All Files.

•   To view all your managed files in the center panel, right-click in the left panel and select Show All Files.

•   If you want to search all your managed files while in Folder Location view, select Show All Files.

•   To find the folder location of a file, click the file's thumbnail in the center panel. The file's folder is highlighted in the left panel.

•   To find files in a specific folder, click the folder in the left panel. Thumbnails for the files in that folder appear in the center panel, grouped under the folder name.

•   To instantly tag files by their folder locations, click the Instant Tag icon in the center panel on the right side of the window. Photoshop Elements will attach tags to the images based on the folder names.

4   To manage files and folders, select a folder and do any of the following:

•   To move a file to a different folder, drag the file's thumbnail from the center panel to a folder in the left panel. Click OK to the message that appears.

•   To view the folder in Windows Explorer, right-click in the left panel and choose Reveal in Explorer.

•   To add or remove the folder from watched-folder status, right-click in the left panel and choose Add to Watched Folders or Remove from Watched Folders.

•   To add a file in the folder to your catalog, right-click in the left panel and choose Add Unmanaged Files to Catalog.

•   To rename the folder, right-click in the left panel and choose Rename Folder. Then type a new name.

•   To delete the folder, right-click in the left panel and choose Delete Folder.

Applying tags to photos

Tags and tag categories are search criteria—sometimes referred to as keywords—that you apply to images. In this example, you'll apply a couple of tags from the default set to one of the images you imported into your catalog.

1 In the shortcuts bar, click Photo Browser, and make sure that Date (Newest First) is selected in the lower left corner of the Organizer window.

2 In the Tags palette, select the Places category tag, and drag it to the thumbnail that shows people looking over a river gorge.

3 Click the arrow next to the People category to expand it so that you can see the Family and Friends sub-categories.

4 Drag the Family subcategory tag to the same thumbnail showing the people by the river gorge.

5 Allow the cursor to rest for a few seconds over the tag icon in the river-gorge thumbnail until a tip appears, identifying the tags that are applied to the image.

Creating new categories and sub-categories

You can add or delete new tag categories and sub-categories to meet your needs.

1 In the Tags palette, click New and choose New Category.

2 In the Create Category window, type **Animals**, and select the bird symbol under Category Icon. Click OK.

3   In the Tags palette, click to select the People category, then click New at the top of the Tags palette, and choose New SubCategory.

4   In the Create Sub-Category window, type **Strangers** in the Sub-Category Name field. Make sure that People is shown in the Parent Category or Sub-Category field, and click OK.

The new tag category and sub-category become part of this catalog.

Applying and editing category assignments

You can add tags to several files at one time, and you can also delete tags from an image.

1   In the thumbnails, click to select the picture of the hummingbirds, then press and hold the Ctrl key and click the seagull picture to select it, too. Both the hummingbirds and seagull pictures should be selected.

2   Drag the Animals tag to either one of the two selected bird thumbnails. The tag is applied to both pictures.

3   Drag the Strangers sub-category tag to the river-gorge image. It is not necessary to select the thumbnail or to deselect the other two thumbnails.

4   Select the river-gorge thumbnail, and choose Window > Properties to open the Properties palette.

   You can also display properties by clicking the Show or Hide Properties ( ) icon at the bottom of the Organizer window.

5   If necessary, select Tags (📷) in the Properties palette to see which tags are applied to this image.

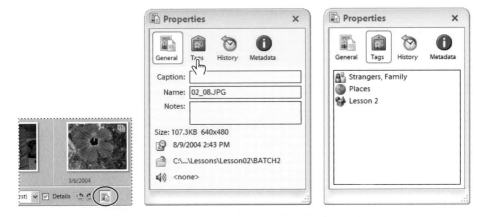

6   Remove the Family tag from the river-gorge image by doing one of the following:

• Right-click the People tag and choose Remove Family sub-category tag.

• In the Properties palette, right-click the Family, Strangers listing and choose Remove Family sub-category tag.

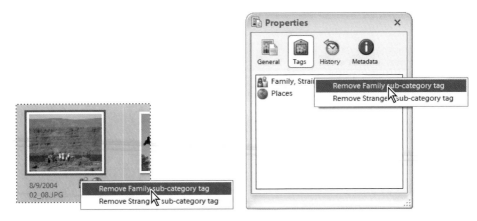

7   Close the Properties palette by clicking the Close button in the upper right corner of the palette or by clicking the Show or Hide Properties button again.

Creating and applying new tags

In the previous topic, you created new tag categories and subcategories. In this topic, you'll create a new tag and specify its location.

1   In the Tags palette, click New, and choose New Tag. The Create Tag window appears.

2   In the Create Tag window, choose Other for category and type **Architecture** for Name, then click OK.

3   Drag the Architecture tag to the ornate Victorian building picture taken April 8, 2003.

The image of the building becomes the tag icon because it's the first image to get this tag.

4   Drag the Architecture tag to the Ferris wheel and the multi-angled glass interior. Three images now have the Architecture tag applied to them.

Converting tags and categories

It's easy to change the hierarchy of categories and tags, promoting or demoting them whenever you like. Doing this does not remove the tags or categories from the images to which you've assigned them.

1   In the Tags palette, drag the Animals category to the Other category.

Now the Animals category appears as a sub-category under Other. Because it's no longer a category, it has the generic sub-category icon instead of the bird icon.

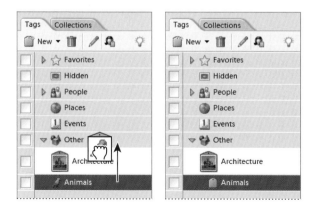

2   Under the People category, right-click the Strangers sub-category, and choose Change Strangers sub-category to a tag from the context menu.

3   In the Tags palette, select the Strangers tag, and click Edit (✐) at the top of the Tags palette.

4   In the Edit Tag window, click the Edit Icon button to open the Edit Tag Icon dialog box.

5   Drag the corners of the boundary in the thumbnail so that it surrounds just the group of people in the image.

6   Click OK to close the window and click OK again to close the Edit Tag window.

Applying more tags to images

There are a few simple ways to automatically tag multiple images, as well as manual methods you can use for applying custom tags.

1   In the Photo Browser Arrangement drop-down menu in the lower left corner of the Organizer window, choose Folder Location.

2   Click Instant Tag on the right end of the separator bar above the thumbnails of BATCH1.

3   In the Create and Apply New Tag dialog box, choose Other in the Category drop-down menu, leaving BATCH1 for Name, and then click OK.

4   Repeat Steps 2 and 3 for the other folder groups, BATCH2 and BATCH3. Click OK.

5   Switch back to Date (Newest First) view, using the same menu you used in Step 1.

6   Click and drag to apply the Strangers tag to any image picturing a person you don't know.

7   (Optional) Create and apply any other tags or categories you might want. For example, you could create a Flowers or Fishing tag, category, or sub-category.

Creating a tag for working files

You can create a tag to apply to your work files throughout the book as you save them in the Organizer.

1 Click Photo Browser (⊞) on the Photoshop Elements shortcuts bar to switch to the Organizer. If Back to All Photos appears above the thumbnails area, select it.

2 In the Tags palette, choose New > New Category on the drop-down menu.

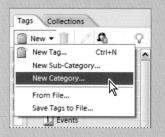

3 In the Create Category dialog box, type **Work Files** *as the Category name, and select one of the Category icons. You can scroll to the right to see other icons. Click OK.*

Using tags to find pictures

Why create and apply all these tags? Because they make it amazingly simple to find your pictures.

1 Click the empty Find box next to the Architecture tag. A binoculars icon appears in the Find box to remind you that it is selected. Only the three thumbnails tagged with the Architecture tag are displayed.

2 Leave the Architecture tag selected. Click the Find box for the BATCH2 tag. Only two thumbnails appear: the two tagged with both the Architecture and BATCH2 tags.

3 In the Matching check boxes above the thumbnails, select Not and then click Best to deselect it. The thumbnails display changes, showing only images that are not tagged for either Architecture or BATCH2.

4   Click Back to All Photos to display all images.

Automatically finding faces for tagging

When you use the Find Faces for Tagging command, Photoshop Elements isolates and displays faces in photos so that you can quickly tag them. This makes it easy to tag faces of friends or family members. Thumbnails of individual faces appear in the Face Tagging window, where you can apply existing tags, or create and apply new tags. As you apply tags to faces in the Face Tagging window, Photoshop Elements removes those faces, making it easier to find and tag the remaining faces. You can select Show Already Tagged Faces if you want the faces to remain after you tag them.

A. Select to show faces already tagged or deselect to hide those faces. B. Tags and tag options. C. Recently used tags. D. Full context image of the most recently selected face.

1   Select the photo of the two boys in the Photo Browser section of the Organizer.

2   Choose Find > Find Faces for Tagging.

Note: If you press Ctrl as you choose Find > Find Faces for Tagging, Photoshop Elements will produce more accurate results (for example, it will find more faces in the background of a busy photo), but it will take longer for the faces to appear.

Photoshop Elements 4.0 processes the photos and searches for faces. Thumbnails of the faces display in the Face Tagging dialog box.

3 In the Find Faces for Tagging window, drag the Family tag onto a face or drag the face onto a Family tag. You can apply other tags in the same manner, and you can select and apply tags to multiple images.

4 Click Done.

You'll use tags throughout this book as a way to locate and organize lesson files.

To find photos by visual similarity

You can search for images containing similar images, color, or general appearance.

1 Select the large pink flower image.

2 Drag the image to the find bar.

Photos with similar visual appearance are displayed in decreasing order of similarity. A similarity percentage appears in the bottom left corner of each image.

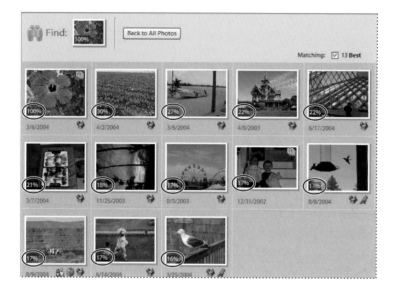

Using photo mail

Have you ever had to wait for an incoming e-mail to download, only to find that the large file contained a single photograph? You can avoid this inconvenience by using the Organizer e-mail function, which creates an optimized version of the image that is designed specifically for sending via e-mail.

1   Select the thumbnail of the tourists looking at the river gorge.

2   On the shortcuts bar, click Share (📷) and choose E-mail.

Note: A dialog box appears in which you can select a preferred e-mail application and you may need to enter your user name and e-mail address, if necessary.

3   In the Attach Selected Items to E-mail window, click the Edit Contacts button.

4   In the Edit Contacts window, click the new contact button (👤) and type in the first and last names (or a nickname—our example uses Mom) of the person to whom you want to send the picture, and the person's e-mail address. Click OK to close the New Contact dialog box and click OK again to close the Contact Book.

5   In the Attach Selected Items to E-mail window, select Individual Attachments from the drop-down menu under Choose Format.

6 Under Select Size and Quality, select Very Small (320 x 240).

This reduces the file size to about 46 KB. It also reduces the download time to 16 seconds for a typical 56 Kbps dial-up modem.

7 Under Message, select and delete the "Here are the photos...." text, and type a message of your own, such as the one shown in the illustration. Then click Next.

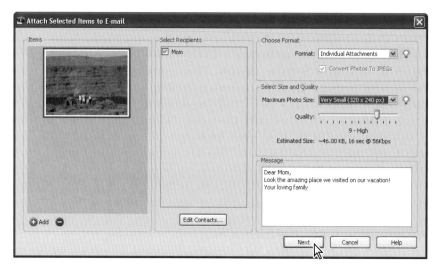

Your default e-mail application immediately creates an e-mail message. You can edit the message and Subject line to say what you want. When you are finished and ready to send the e-mail, make sure that you are connected to the Internet, either click Send if you want to send an actual e-mail or close the message without saving or sending it.

Using an online sharing service

You can use Adobe Photoshop Services in Photoshop Elements to send images and creations to online service providers. You can also use the services to get photos.

1 Select the photos you wish to share.

2 In the Photo Browser or Date View, choose Share > Share Online... from the shortcuts bar to access the Kodak® EasyShare Gallery.

3 Create a new user account by filling out the required fields, and click Next.

4 Click to select the Add New Address option.

5   Complete the address information for the person with whom you will share the photos, then click Next.

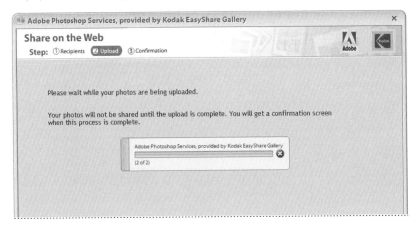

6   Select the address book check box and type **Photos** in the subject field and type **Enjoy!** in the message field. Click Next.

7   Click Done or Click Order Prints if you want to purchase prints of your photos, and then follow the on-screen directions.

Printing

The Organizer helps you reduce waste of expensive photographic paper. You can print single or multiple images on the same page, arranging them on the paper in the sizes you want.

1   Choose Edit > Select All to select all the thumbnails if you want to print them all. Or, click one thumbnail to select it, and then hold down Ctrl and click several others to print selected images.

2   Choose File > Print.

3   In the Print Selected Photos dialog box, make the following adjustments:

• Select an available printer.

• Under Select Type of Print, leave Individual Prints selected.

• Under Select Print Size and Options, select 3.5" x 5".

If a warning appears about print resolution, click OK to close it. Some of the sample files are provided at a low resolution.

- Click the One Photo Per Page option to deselect it, removing the check mark.

4 (Optional) Do any of the following:

- On the left side of the dialog box, select one of the thumbnails and then click Remove (⊖) at the bottom of the thumbnails column to remove that image from the set that will be printed.

- Click Add (⊕) under the column of thumbnails. Select the Entire Catalog option, and then click the check box of any image that you want to add to the set to be printed. Click Done.

- Under the Print Preview in the middle of the dialog box, click the arrows to see the other pages that will be printed.

Note: You can select only images that are part of the current catalog. If you want to add other pictures to the printing batch, you must first add them to the catalog, using one of the methods described earlier in this lesson.

5   Do one of the following:

• Click Cancel to close the dialog box without printing. This is recommended if you want to save your ink and paper for your own images.

• Click Print to actually print the pictures.

To print a contact sheet

Contact sheets let you easily preview groups of images by displaying a series of thumbnail images on a single page.

1   In the Photo Browser, select one or more photos.

2   Choose File > Print.

Note: If you don't select specific photos before choosing Print, Photoshop Elements asks whether you want to print all photos in the Photo Browser.

3   In the Print Selected Photos dialog box, choose a printer from the Select Printer menu.

4   Choose Contact Sheet from the Select Type of Print menu. The preview layout automatically uses all photos listed on the left side of the Print Photos or Print Selected Photos dialog box.

To remove a photo, select its thumbnail and click the Remove button.

5   For Columns, type **4** to specify the number of columns in the layout. You can specify between 1 and 9 columns.

The thumbnail size and number of rows are adjusted according to your choice. If the number of photos listed in the Print Photos dialog box exceeds the capacity of a single page, more pages are added to accommodate them.

6   To add text labels below each thumbnail, select any of the following to include these items in the text label for each image:

• Date, to print the date embedded in the image.

• Caption, to print the caption text embedded in the file's metadata.

• Filename, to print the image file name.

• Page Numbers, to print page numbers at the bottom of each page if multiple contact sheets are printed.

Note: Words in the text label may be truncated, depending on the page setup and layout.

7 Click Print to print or Click Cancel.

To burn photos to CD or DVD

Use the Burn command to copy a set of photos to a CD or DVD. For instance, you might want to give your photos to a friend, or create a backup copy of your images.

1 Make sure you have a CD or DVD drive with writable media connected to your computer.

2 In the Photo Browser, select the items you want to copy or move.

3 Choose File > Burn.

The Burn/Backup wizard appears. If you haven't selected any files, you'll see a dialog box giving you the option of selecting all files in the Photo Browser.

4 Select Copy/Move files, then click Next.

5 Check Copy/Move All Files in the Version Set and click Next.

Note: Choosing the Move Files option deletes the original files from your hard disk after they are copied to a CD or DVD.

6 Click Done.

Congratulations! You've finished the lesson, and we're hoping that you feel pretty good about your accomplishment.

In this lesson, you've imported files into the Organizer using various techniques. You've used several handy tools for quickly completing basic editing tasks. You have seen how you can share images by e-mail, and how to set up single or multiple images for printing. Finally, you've created, edited, and applied tags to individual photographs so that they'll be easy to find in future work sessions.

Review

▶ **Review questions**

1   How do you open the Organizer component of Adobe Photoshop Elements 4.0?

2   What's the fastest way to add all the images on your computer to your Organizer catalog, regardless of where they are located in your folder structure?

3   Name several ways you can make it easier to find specific photos in your catalog.

4   How do you print multiple images on a single sheet of paper?

5   Why should you use the Organizer to prepare photos for e-mail?

▶ **Review answers**

1   There are several ways to open the Organizer. You can select View and Organize Photos on the Welcome Screen when you start Photoshop Elements 4.0. Or, if the Photoshop Elements Editor is already open, you can select Photo Browser at the top of the work area. If you always want to open Photoshop Elements in the Organizer, use the Start Up In drop-down menu in the lower left border of the Welcome Screen to choose the Organizer.

2   The most effortless way to catalog all your images is to choose File > Get Photos > By Searching, and then selecting your hard disk for Look In. This method collects all images, regardless of how disorganized they might be in your folders.

3   You can find photos by file location, by date, by import batch, and by using tags. The drop-down menu in the lower left corner of the Organizer determines the order in which the thumbnails appear, such as Date (Newest First) or File Location. For a calendar view of your images, click Date View on the shortcuts bar. You can also use the Find menu, which offers many more ways to set search criteria. Select Find boxes for a tag to limit the thumbnail display to images with that tag.

4   All multi-photo printing with Photoshop Elements is done in the Organizer, although you can start the process in the Editor, too. You start by selecting the photo or photos you want to print, and choosing File > Print. Then deselect One Photo Per Page.

5   The Organizer feature for attaching photos to e-mail creates and attaches versions of your photos that are sized appropriately for e-mail. This means it's faster to send them, and faster for others to download them.

3 | Sharing Creations

Slide shows and other projects, called Photo Creations, are ways that you can present and share images from your Organizer catalog. You may want to build creations for several reasons: to share your photos online, to create a slide show VCD (video CD) for your friends and family, or perhaps, even to print your own coffee-table book. A slide show is fun to build because it allows you to combine images, music, narration, and text to create a unique multimedia display.

In this lesson, you'll learn how to do the following:

- Create a photo slide show from available media.
- Add text to create titles and captions.
- Add a soundtrack and narration to liven up your slide show.
- Export your creation to share with family and friends.

Before you begin, make sure that you've correctly copied the project files from the Adobe Photoshop Elements 4.0 Classroom in a Book CD (attached to the inside of the back cover of this book). See "Copying the Classroom in a Book files" on page 3.

Slide show creation workflow

When creating a slide show, you'll follow this basic workflow:

- Define overall slide show preferences.
- Add visual media to your slide show.
- Add text and graphics.
- Add transitions and effects to your slides.
- Add audio media (a soundtrack or narration).
- Output your slide show.

Getting started

In this lesson, you'll use the catalog you created at the start of the book. If the CIB Catalog is already open, you can skip these steps and move on to the next section, "What is Media."

1 Start Photoshop Elements. On the Welcome Screen, select View and Organize Photos. If the CIB Catalog is open, skip to "What is Media." If the CIB Catalog is not open, complete the following steps.

2 Choose File > Catalog.

3 In the Catalog dialog box, click Open.

4 In the Open Catalog dialog box, select the CIB Catalog.psa file (or, if you renamed the file in "Getting Started," select that file), and click Open.

If you do not see the CIB Catalog file, review the procedures found in "Getting Started." See "Copying the Lessons files from the CD" on page 3, and "Reconnecting missing files to a catalog" on page 7.

What is media?

Photoshop Elements slide show media can be any combination of still images, video, audio, text, and graphics. Photoshop Elements 4.0 supports the following file formats: for image formats, .jpg, .jpe, .jpeg, .png, .tif, .tiff, .psd, and .pdd; for video formats, .avi, .mpg, .mpeg, .mpe, and .wmv; for audio formats, .mp3, .wav, and .wma.

Using the Slide Show Editor

The Slide Show Editor allows you to create, edit, and save your slide show projects with ease and efficiency.

1   Launch Adobe Photoshop Elements 4.0 and select Make Photo Creations from the Welcome Screen. This opens the creation setup window.

Note: If you are already working in the Organizer, you can open the Creations window from the file menu by choosing File > Create > New Creation...

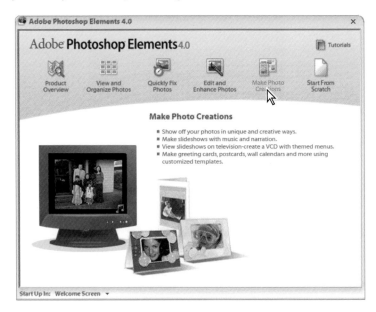

2 Choose Slide Show from the list of creations at the left of the creation setup window, then click OK to begin working on your slide show.

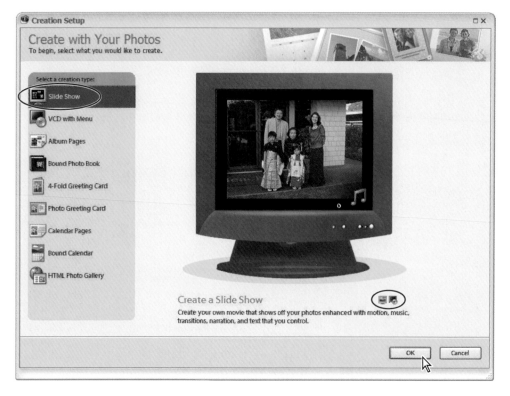

Note: If you click on the various types of creations you can build with Photoshop Elements, you will notice that the main screen image changes to give you a preview of what each project will look like. Below the preview are numerous small icons. Place your cursor over them, and you should see a dialog explaining what each icon means. These icons show the output possibilities for each type of creation. You will notice that slide shows can either be viewed on a computer or burned to a VCD to view on a television.

3 Choose OK from the Slide Show Preferences window that appears, accepting the default settings.

You can use the Slide Show Preferences window to define the parameters of the overall slide show, such as how long each slide is visible, what type of transition is used between the slides, and how the soundtrack behaves. All these setting are also available individually from inside the Slide Show Editor itself.

4 Click the Add Media button at the top of the Slide Show Editor, then select the "Photos and Videos from Folder" option. Navigate to the Lesson03 folder that you copied from the *Photoshop Elements Classroom in a Book* CD.

There are two ways to bring media into the Slide Show Editor. You can select the media either from the organizer or from a folder.

5   Select all the images in the airshow folder by clicking on the first image, holding the Shift key and clicking on the last image. Click the Open button to import these pictures into your storyboard.

Selecting files for the slide show. Your image files may look different in this window, depending upon your windows preferences.

Note: *You can also select a series of images by holding down the Ctrl key and clicking on the files you wish to select.*

You may need to resize your Slide Show Editor in order to see the storyboard icons at the bottom.

6   Click the Play button in your workspace to preview your slide show.

You will notice that each slide holds for a few seconds and then gradually fades into the next slide in the storyboard. This is because we left the preferences set to the default of a five-second hold with a fade transition. We will edit this later in the lesson.

7   Click the Pause button to pause the slide show.

Note: *While the slide show is playing, the Play button becomes the Pause button.*

8   Click Save Project in the upper left corner of the Slide Show Editor. In the project window, name your project **air show** and click Save.

All photo creations are accessible through the Organizer.

Adding text

Slide shows are not limited to images. You can use the Photoshop elements text tools to add both titles and captions to your work. The Text tool is accessible from the "Extras" menu on your Palette Bin.

1   Click on the first slide in your storyboard to make it visible in your work area.

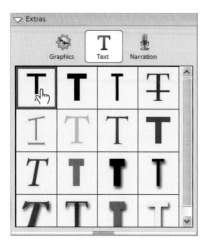

2   From your Palette Bin, click on the Text tool to activate it. From the group of text styles that are displayed, choose the option in the upper left corner.

3   Click and drag the text style icon onto your slide and position it in the upper right corner. This creates a text frame in your work area. The text frame that you create will have the generic phrase "Your text here." You will change the text in the next step.

Note: *You can double-click the text style from the Palette Bin to create a text frame in the center of your work area.*

4   Double-click the text frame that you created in the previous step to open the text editor. In the editor, type in the phrase **Off we go into the wild blue yonder**, and click OK.

5   Reposition your text to center it in the top of the image by clicking and dragging while your cursor is over the text frame.

6   With your text frame highlighted, the Properties palette in the Palette Bin displays the parameters for editing text. Click the drop shadow icon, adding this style to the text.

Using the text Properties palette, you can change the font, size, color, opacity, alignment, and style of the text. The Properties palette is contextual, and changes depending on the type of object you have selected. When text is selected, you have access to text properties. When an image or transition is selected, other properties are displayed.

Using the Palette Bin

The palette bin provides a convenient location to store and manage the palettes you use for editing images. By default, the How To, Styles and Effects, and Layers palettes are located in the Palette Bin. Other palettes you open (using the Window menu) are positioned in the work area–this is known as floating. You can change which palettes float and which are stored in the Palette Bin.

To remove palettes from the Palette Bin or close palettes:

1 Drag a palette out of the Palette Bin by clicking and dragging the title bar which lists the name of the palette.

2 Click the More button on the palette to open the palette menu, and deselect Place in Palette Bin when Closed option.

(continued)

Using the Palette Bin *(continued)*

3 *To close a palette, click its close box (⊠) on the palette title bar, or choose Window > [palette name] to close it. Palettes that display a check mark adjacent to their name in the Window menu are visible, selecting a palette name that includes a check mark causes the palette window to close.*

To add floating palettes to the Palette Bin

1 *Choose Window > [palette name] to open the palette you want to place in the Palette Bin.*

2 *Drag the palette by its tab to the Palette Bin. The tab contains the palette name, and is not the colored bar above the name.*

You can also choose the Place in Palette Bin when Closed option and close the palette window.

To adjust palette sizes in the Palette Bin

Adjust the height of palettes by doing either or both of the following:

- Click the triangle to the left of the palette name to minimize or expand each palette as needed.

- Click and drag the separator bars between palettes up or down to adjust the height of a palette.

Adding graphics

Adobe Photoshop Elements 4.0 comes complete with a set of ready-to-use graphics that you can use to add a flair to your projects. Like your Text tool, graphics are located in the extras tab of your Palette Bin.

1 Click on slide three in your storyboard to load it into your work area.

2 From your Palette Bin, click on the Graphics tool to activate it. Scroll toward the bottom of the group under the miscellaneous section and select the rocket ship. Click and drag the rocket ship onto your slide and position it as shown in the image below.

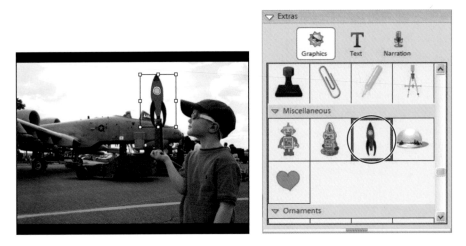

Notice that with a graphic selected, the Properties palette changes to display the parameters that are available for working with graphics. If desired, you can alter the size of a graphic and apply graphic styles to it.

Applying transitions

When you set the slide show preferences for this project, the transition for all the slides was set as a fade. As you preview the show, you may want to vary the transitions from one slide to another. Changing transitions is easy to do using the storyboard and Properties palette. The number and types of properties that you can edit depends on the specific transitions. One common parameter among all transitions is duration. Transitions are denoted on your storyboard by the small boxes between the slides. The icon inside the box indicates which transition you are using, for example the fade transition is symbolized by an overlapping A/B.

1   Click on transition 1, which is located between the first and second slides in your storyboard.

2   In the Properties palette, click on the Transition drop-down menu and select "Wipe" from the list. This pops up a secondary property, Direction. Click the Direction drop-down and set it to be the second option, top to bottom.

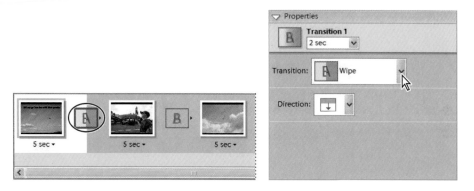

You may have noticed that one of the transitions you can choose is Random. This setting causes the slide show to play any one of the available transitions.

3   Click on the Duration drop-down menu and select 3 seconds to create a slower transition.

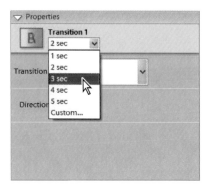

To create a transition longer than 5 seconds select Custom. The duration is always measured in seconds and cannot be longer than 60 seconds.

4   Change other transitions by selecting them and changing their properties.

You can hold down the Ctrl key to select multiple transitions at once and edit them as a group.

Panning and zooming

Pan and zoom refer to the movement of a camera with the subject. In Photoshop Elements, the Pan & Zoom options allow you to simulate the appearance of camera movement over a still image. This technique can be used to add emphasis and liven up an otherwise static image.

Note: The Pan & Zoom effect is not supported by some slide show output types, most notably PDF output.

1   Click slide two in your storyboard to load it into your project window.

2   Click the Enable Pan & Zoom checkbox in the Properties palette.

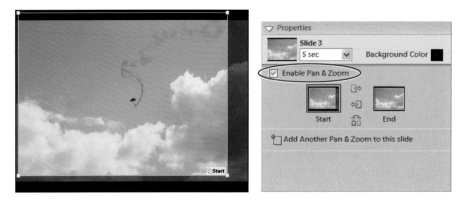

3   A bounding box labeled "Start" appears in your work area. This indicates the start position of the Pan & Zoom effect. Scale this bounding box by dragging with your cursor at one of its corner points. Move the bounding box by positioning your cursor inside of it and dragging. Position it so that it matches the figure below, outlining the skydiver.

4   Click the End thumbnail in your Properties palette and position its bounding box to enclose the entire frame, as seen in the image below.

5   Preview your slide show by clicking the Play button at the bottom of the work area.

You've added a simple animated effect using the Pan & Zoom feature. Now you'll add a second Pan & Zoom effect on the same image. After you've finished previewing the slide show, click the Pause button.

6   Click slide two in your storyboard, and in your Properties palette, click the Add Another Pan & Zoom to this slide checkbox.

This adds a copy of the slide to your storyboard and links the copy to the original. The start point of the second Pan & Zoom effect is automatically created from the end point of the previous one.

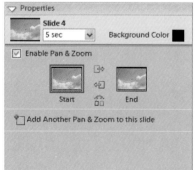

7   Click the End point thumbnail in your Properties palette and position its bounding box to enclose only the skydiver as seen in the image below.

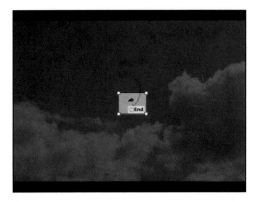

8   Click the Play button to preview your slide show.

The Pan & Zoom now begins and ends with a close up of the skydiver.

Reordering slides

When you first added the slides to your project, you did not have the opportunity to set their order. It is often necessary to change the order of the slides to fit the story you are telling. There are three simple and easy ways to set the order of the slides:

Slide Order drop-down menu—Click on the Slide Order drop-down menu in the upper right corner of your storyboard to choose one of the auto-sorting methods for your slides: from the Organizer, date-based, random, or folder location.

Drag and drop on the storyboard—On your storyboard, click on slide five and drag it to the right past slide six. When a vertical blue bar appears, release the slide. You have changed the slide order.

Quick reorder—The quick reorder menu is the best way for changing the order of multiple slides since it allows you to view your entire slide show at once.

1   Click the Quick Reorder button located to the upper left of your storyboard.

2   In the window that appears, drag and drop slides to change their position. You can use the Shift or Ctrl keys on your keyboard to select multiple slides.

Click the Back button when finished editing to return to the main Slide Show Editor.

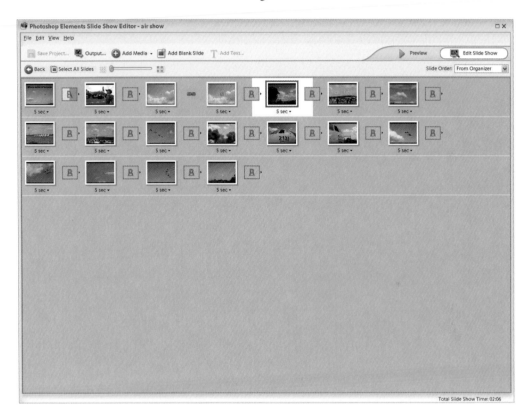

Adding audio

You can easily add an audio file that plays in the background of your slide show, using the Add Media button. Audio plays as your slide show progresses, and automatically stops at the end of the show.

1   Click the Add Media button (⊕) at the top of the Slide Show Editor to add an audio file to your slide show.

2   Select the Audio from Folder option and navigate to the Lesson03 folder.

3   Select the soundtrack_01.wav file and click the Open button. Your soundtrack is added to your storyboard and placed just below your slides.

Note: Depending on your Windows preferences, the file extension .wav may not be visible.

4   Click on soundtrack_01.wav on your storyboard to view its properties in the
Properties palette. The slide show duration is visible in the lower right corner of the
Slide Show Editor interface. You may need to maximize the window size in order to see
the duration information. The audio track is a few seconds longer than the slide show
itself.

5   Adjust the duration of the soundtrack by clicking and dragging the end slider to the
left, matching the duration of the slide show.

Adding narration (optional)

If you have a microphone attached to your computer, you can use it to add a narration
to one or more slides in your project. Unlike background audio, the narration track is
attached to each slide and will automatically change the slide's duration, if necessary.
The narration interface looks very similar to a standard tape recorder, with controls to
record, stop, and play along; with controls for inserting saved audio tracks as narrations,
and deleting saved narration tracks.

1   From your Palette Bin, click on the Narration button

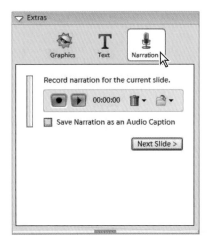

2   Click to select the slide you would like to narrate, then click the red record button. When you are finished with your narration, click the Stop button.

Adding narration can increase the duration of the slide. If your narration is longer than the slide's display duration, Photoshop Elements will automatically increase the slide's display length.

3   Click the Play button to listen to the narration you have just created. If you are happy with it, move on to the next slide. If you want to change the narration, click the trash can icon to delete it.

Note: If you are using a soundtrack with your slide show, it can interfere with the viewer's ability to hear the narration. If the soundtrack is too loud, you will have to go back to its parameters and lower the volume.

Adding a title

Blank slides can be used as placeholders for graphics, to create a dramatic effect, or to create a title screen.

1   Click to select the first slide in your storyboard.

2   Click the Add Blank Slide button at the top of the Slide Show Editor.

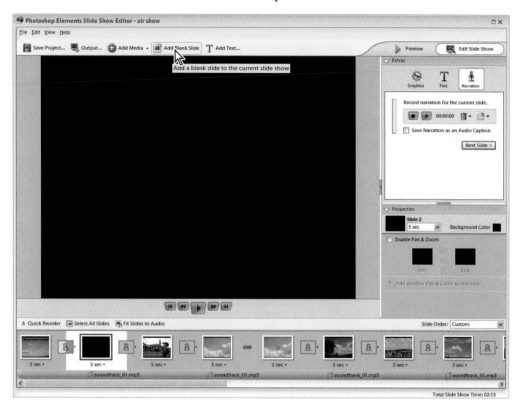

The slide becomes the second slide in your show. Blank slides are automatically added after whichever slide was selected in your storyboard.

3   Drag slide one to the right to move the blank slide to the front of your show.

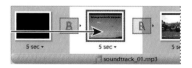

4   Click the blank slide to display it in the work area, then click to select the Text tool from the Palette Bin.

5   Drag a text slide into the slide work area.

6   Change the text color to white by clicking the Color square to the right of the Color option in the Properties palette. In the Color Picker window, click the white color in the upper left corner of the area labeled "select color" then click OK.

7   Double-click the text frame and enter the text **A Day at the AIR SHOW**.

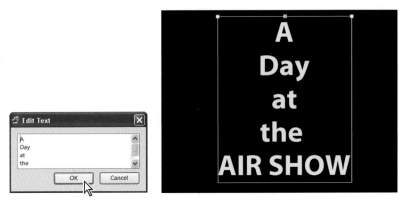

A title does not have to be created on a blank slide. You can also create a title using Photoshop Elements in editing mode, which you will learn in Lesson 7, "Working with Text."

8   Click OK to close the Edit Text window.

Choosing an output option

Once you have finished creating a slide show, you can distribute it to your audience. Photoshop Elements 4.0 supports a variety of distribution methods. There are four export categories: Save As a File, Burn to Disk, E-mail Slide Show, Send to TV. The Send to TV option requires Windows XP Media Center Edition.

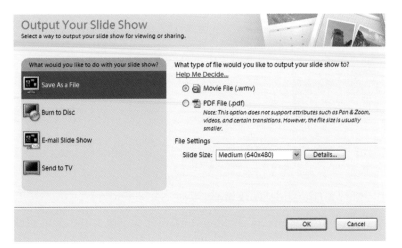

Save As a File

Save As a File saves the slide show as either a Windows Media Video (.wmv) or a Portable Document Format (.PDF) file. For the WMV format, you must specify a file size. Larger sizes equate to larger but better quality images. The PDF option does not support certain slide show features, most notably, Pan & Zoom, and some transitions will appear different, such as the clock wipe which becomes a fade when converted to PDF.

1 From the File drop-down menu, select Output Slide Show.

2 From the output menu, choose the .wmv format.

This will create a video file that will be compatible with most Windows-based computers and will play in the Windows media player.

3 From the file settings drop-down menu select Medium (640x480) as your slide size.

The output size of your slide show is very important. Larger sizes tend to look better and give you a cleaner video image but they will always produce files that take up more disk space and are therefore more difficult to send to friends and family. The medium setting is a good compromise between disk usage and quality. You can always click on the Details button to see information about the setting you have chosen.

4 Click OK and choose a location on your hard drive to save your video. By default, the name of your video file will be the same as that of your slide show, but you can specify a new name if you prefer.

By default, the program will want to save in your "My Videos" folder which is located on your hard drive in your "My Documents" folder. But you can specify a new location if you like.

5 Click Save and Photoshop Elements will begin to build (a process called rendering) your video file.

Rendering the video files is a very intensive process that will take up a considerable amount of your system resources. Your hardware configuration will determine how quickly your video file is produced.

6 When your file has finished rendering, a message will pop up asking you if you would like to import it into your catalog. Choose yes and your video file will now be accessible through your Organizer.

7 Close the slide show. It is not necessary to save your work.

Burn to Disk

Burn to Disk allows you to burn the slide show to either a VCD (video CD) or DVD for display on a standard console DVD player, depending on your hardware configuration. To create a VCD which can play on most modern DVD players, you would need a drive capable of burning CD-ROMS. For the DVD, you need a DVD burner.

E-mail Slide Show

E-mail Slide Show has the same format options as Save as File. Additionally, the slide show will give you the option of attaching it to an e-mail message.

Send to TV

As the name implies, this export format lets you watch your slide show on your television directly from your computer. You need to have Windows XP Media Center Edition for this option to work.

Browsing photos using Windows Media Center Edition

If you have Microsoft® Windows® XP® Media Center Edition 2005 installed, you can view and share your photos on a connected standard or high definition television, or another compatible display device connected to a Media Center Extender. Refer to the documentation that came with your computer, television, or other device for more information.

Use the remote control for your Media Center device to view photos and choose options.

Photoshop Elements supports Microsoft Windows XP Media Center Edition 2005 only.

Working with Premiere Elements

Adobe Premiere Elements software offers the perfect combination of creative control and reliability for home video editing. Premiere Elements makes it easy to tell the stories you want to tell, by automating tedious tasks so you're free to create cool effects and transitions. And when you have finished with your creation, you can easily export it for viewing on a computer or DVD.

Video from Premiere can be used in your slide shows, or you could create titles and graphics for your Premiere movie in Photoshop. More information can be found in the *Adobe Premiere Elements Classroom in a Book*.

Review

▶ **Review questions**

1   How do you begin the slide show creation process in Photoshop Elements?

2   How would you change the duration or type of a transition?

3   What are the four output options available for your slide shows?

▶ **Review answers**

1   From the Organizer, select the "create" button to open the new creations window. You can also open the new creations window from the file menu by selecting File > Create > Slide Show.

2   Select the transition that you want to edit from the storyboard. The transitions properties are visible in the lower section of your Palette Bin.

3   Save As a File, Burn to Disk, E-mail Slide Show, and Send to TV.

4 | Adjusting Color in Images

Unwanted color casts can be introduced into your images because of poor lighting or the type of input device used. In this lesson, you will learn how to adjust for these color casts.

In this lesson, you will learn how to do the following:

- Auto-correct images from either Quick Fix or Standard Edit mode.

- Use individual automatic options to improve images.

- Adjust skin tones.

- Correct an image using Smart Fix.

- Apply the Color Variations feature to shift color balance.

- Fix red eye reflections, both manually and automatically.

- Replace the color of a pictured object with another color.

- Make and save selection areas for future use.

- Troubleshoot common problems when printing color pictures.

- Work with color management.

This lesson shows you many different ways to change the color balance in your pictures, beginning with the one-step correction features. From there, you'll discover advanced features and adjustment techniques that can be mastered easily.

Most people need at least an hour and a half to complete the work in this lesson. The work involves several independent projects, so you can do them all in one session or in several sessions.

In this lesson, you will use the CIB Catalog you created earlier in the book. If necessary, open this catalog by choosing File > Catalog in Organizer mode, then click Open.

This lesson assumes that you are already familiar with the overall features of the Photoshop Elements 4.0 work area and recognize the two ways in which you can use Photoshop Elements: the Editor and the Organizer. This lesson focuses primarily on the Editor. Lesson 4 also builds on the skills and concepts covered in Lessons 1, 2, and 3. If you need to learn more about these items, see Photoshop Elements Help.

If you haven't already copied the project files from the CD attached to the inside back cover of this book, do so now. See "Copying the Classroom in a Book files" on page 3.

Note: As you gain advanced skills in Photoshop Elements 4.0, you may require additional information about issues and problems. For help with common problems you might have when completing lessons in this book, see "Why won't Photoshop Elements do what I tell it to do?" later in this lesson.

Getting started

Before you start working on files, take a few moments to make sure that your work area and palettes are set up to match the illustrations shown for these projects.

1   Start Photoshop Elements in Standard Edit mode by selecting Edit and Enhance Photos in the Photoshop Elements Welcome Screen. If the Organizer is already open, click and hold on the Edit button (🖼) and release on Go to Standard Edit.

2 In Standard Edit, use the Window menu to make the Layers, Styles and Effects, Navigator, and Undo History palettes visible. In both Standard Edit and Quick Fix, collapsed palettes can be expanded by clicking the arrow beside the palette name on the palette title bar.

Note: For instructions on how to add or remove palettes from the Standard Edit Palette Bin, see "Using the Palette Bin" in Lesson 3, "Sharing Creations." You cannot add or remove palettes in Quick Fix mode.

Palette Bin for Standard Edit mode, and for Quick Fix mode.

Now your Palette Bins are set up in both modes for the work you'll do in this lesson. In some procedures, you'll use Quick Fix mode and in others you'll use Standard Edit mode, so it's convenient to set them up ahead of time.

Fixing photographs automatically

You've probably noticed that not all the photographs used for the lesson projects are of professional quality. But that doesn't mean they are not valuable images, or that they don't deserve to be made as good as possible. Many photographs selected for this book typify the challenges ordinary people, with modest camera skills, might face when attempting to make the most of their pictures.

Quick Fix multiple files as a batch

Photoshop Elements can fix photographs without even opening them. In this section, you'll apply automatic fixes to all the image files used in this lesson. You'll save those fixed files as copies of the originals so that you can compare the results at the end of each project.

1   Choose File > Process Multiple Files. The Process Multiple Files window opens.

2   In the Process Multiple Files window, set the source and destination folders as follows:

• For Process Files From, select Folder, if it is not already selected.

• Under Source, make sure Include All Subfolders is deselected. Then click Browse. Find and select the Lesson04 folder in the Lessons folder. Click OK to close the Browse for Folder dialog box.

• Under Destination, click Browse. Then find and select the My CIB Work folder that you created at the start of the book. Click OK to close the Browse for Folder dialog box.

3   Select Rename Files. Type **Autofix_** in the first field, and select Document Name in the second field.

4   Under Quick Fix, on the right side of the dialog box, select all four options: Auto Levels, Auto Contrast, Auto Color, and Sharpen.

5   Review all selections in the dialog box, comparing them to the illustration below. Make sure that there are no check marks for the Resize Images or Convert Files to options.

Note: If an error message appears, saying that some files couldn't be processed, ignore it. This refers to a hidden file that is not an image, so it has no effect on the success of your project. If an error message appears saying that files are missing, that means that the Lessons folder has been moved or was not expanded correctly. See "Copying the Classroom in a Book files" on page 3 and redo that procedure, following the instructions exactly.

6   When you are sure that all selections are correct, click OK.

Photoshop Elements goes to work, automatically opening and closing image windows. All you need to do is sit back and wait for the process to finish.

Note: You can see the Quick Fixed images using Windows Explorer or in Photoshop Elements by clicking on the Photo Browser button to open the Photo Browser. Then find and select the My CIB Work folder in the Folder palette so that the thumbnails for the Quick Fixed files appear in the Photo Browser. For more information on the Photo Browser, see Photoshop Elements Help.

Adding the corrected files to the Organizer

The Save, Save As, and Save Optimized As dialog boxes all have an Include in Organizer option that is selected by default. When you use the Process Multiple Files feature, this option isn't part of the process, so you must do that manually.

Note: You'll need to access the files in the CIB Catalog you created at the start of this book. If this catalog is not open, open the Organizer and then open the CIB Catalog by choosing File > Catalog and clicking Open.

1 Click Photo Browser button ( ) to open the Organizer.

2 Choose File > Get Photos > From Files and Folders.

3 In the dialog box that appears, locate and open the My CIB Work folder.

4 Select the five Autofix_ files by holding down Shift or Ctrl as you click to select all five. Then select Get Photos.
If a red eye message appears, click OK.

5 The Import Attached Tags window opens. Click OK to import the images without tags, as you'll be adding tags manually in the next few steps. The Organizer displays the newly added image thumbnails.
When the Auto Red Eye Fix Complete window appears, click OK. If a message appears reminding you that only the new photos will appear, click OK.

6 Choose Edit > Select All, or press Ctrl+A.

7 Drag the Lesson 4 tag to the thumbnails to apply it.

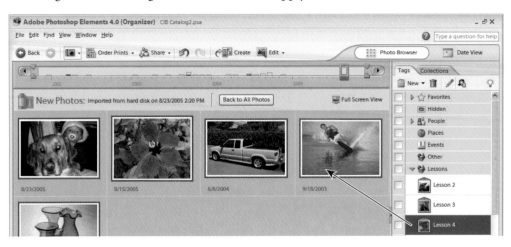

8 Select Back to All Photos.

Now you are ready to discover other methods for correcting color.

Using Quick Fix for editing

Quick Fix conveniently assembles many of the basic photo fixing tools in Photoshop Elements. If one control doesn't work for your image, click the Reset button and try another one. You can also adjust your image using the slider controls, whether you've used the Quick Fix feature or not.

Applying individual automatic adjustments with Quick Fix

When you apply automatic fixes to images using the Process Multiple Files dialog box, you only briefly see the before, during, and after versions of the file.

In this project, you'll apply individual aspects of automatic fixing one at a time. This is useful because it allows you to see how the different phases affect the image, and also enables you to make individual adjustments to the correction process.

Opening image files for Quick Fix editing

You'll use the same technique you learned in Lesson 2 for using the Organizer to find and open files for editing in Quick Fix mode.

1   If the Organizer is no longer forward, switch to it now.

2   In the Tags palette, click the Find box to the left of the Lesson 4 tag.

3   Select the picture of the three vases, 04_01.jpg, to make it active.

Note: To view your file names in the Organizer choose Edit > Preferences > General and select Show File Names in Details.

4   Click Edit (🖎) on the Organizer shortcuts bar, and choose Go to Quick Fix. Unlike Standard Edit mode, the active image file fills the entire work area by default.

5   In the View drop-down menu in the lower left area of the image window, choose Before and After (Portrait).

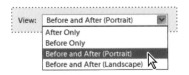

Note: You can change from Before and After (Portrait) to Before and After (Landscape) if that arrangement works better for you. The portrait view shows the before and after versions of the image side by side. The landscape view shows them one above the other.

Using Smart Fix

Assuming Photoshop Elements is still open in Quick Fix mode, you see four palettes—General Fixes, Lighting, Color, and Sharpen, in the Palette Bin on the right. In the General Fixes palette, the first option available is called Smart Fix.

Smart Fix corrects overall color balance and improves shadow and highlight detail in your image. As with other automatic fixes in Quick Fix mode, you can click the Auto button to apply these corrections automatically. You can also move the Smart Fix slider to vary the amount of the adjustment. Or, as in the following steps, you can use a combination of both.

1 In the Palette Bin, under General Fixes, select the Auto button for Smart Fix. Notice the immediate effect on the image.

2 Now move the Smart Fix slider to change the adjustments of the color balance and detail in your image. You can make a determination visually as to which adjustment works best for you. In our example the slider is in the middle.

Note: Use of the other General Fixes control, Red Eye Fix, will be discussed later in this lesson.

Applying other automatic fixes

Additional automatic fixes are available in the Palette Bin.

1 In the Palette Bin, under Lighting, select the Auto button for Levels. Depending upon the adjustment you made in Smart Fix, you may or may not see a big shift in the lighting of this image.

2 One at a time, select the Auto buttons for Contrast, Color, and Sharpen, noticing the difference in the image between each action. You may need to open a palette to see the Auto button.

3 Choose File > Save As. In the Save As dialog box, locate and select the My CIB Work folder, rename the file **04_01_Work**, and save it in the JPEG format. If Save in Version Set with Original is selected, deselect it. Choose Save. When the JPEG Options dialog box appears, select High in the Quality drop-down menu, and click OK.

4 Choose File > Close, to close your file.

Comparing methods of fixing color

The automatic correction features in Photoshop Elements 4.0 do an excellent job of bringing out the best in most photographs. But each photograph is unique, and so are the potential problems. Some photographs don't respond well to automatic fixes and require a more hands-on approach to color correction.

Photoshop Elements 4.0 offers many approaches to color correction. The more approaches you master, the more likely you'll be able meet the challenge of fixing a difficult photograph. In this section, you'll study three different procedures for correcting a color problem and compare the results.

Creating extra working copies of an image

You're going to compare three approaches to color correction, so you'll need three copies of the same photograph.

Note: By now, you've should have mastered the procedure for using tags to locate the files you need in the Organizer. From now on, the instructions for opening files will be summarized rather than explained in detail.

1   If necessary, click the Photo Browser button ( ) on the shortcuts bar to switch to the Organizer, and use the Lesson 4 tag to find the 04_02.jpg file, the photo of the waterskier.

2   Select the image thumbnail. Then click Edit ( ) and choose Go to Quick Fix.

3   In Quick Fix mode of the Editor, choose File > Duplicate. When a message appears, click OK to accept the default name, 04_02 copy.jpg.

4   Repeat Step 3 to create another duplicate, 04_02 copy 2.jpg.

Leave all three copies of the image file open for the next topics. You can tell that all are open because the thumbnails appear in the Photo Bin at the bottom of your screen.

Automatically fixing color

At the beginning of this lesson, you applied all four Quick Fix options to each of the images used in this lesson and saved the results in a separate location. In this procedure, you'll apply just one type of Quick Fix.

1   In the Photo Bin, select the 04_02.jpg thumbnail to make it the active file.

2   In the Color palette, click Auto to fix only the color.

Compare the Before and After views of the file.

3   Choose File > Save, saving the file in the My CIB Work folder and in JPEG format, changing the name to **04_02_Work**. Make sure Save in Version Set with Original is deselected. Click Save, leaving all other options in the Save and JPEG Options dialog box unchanged.

About viewing modes and image window arrangements

When you work in Quick Fix mode, only one image file appears in the work area, regardless of how many files are open. The inactive, open files appear as thumbnails in the Photo Bin but not in the work area.

When you work in Standard Edit mode, other arrangements are possible. You can usually adjust the size and placement of image windows in the work area. If you can't arrange individual windows freely, then your view is probably set to Maximize Mode. If opening or closing some files causes unexpected rearrangements of image windows, your view is probably set to Automatically Tile.

Maximize fills the work area with the active image window, so it's the only image you can see.

Automatically Tile resizes and arranges all open images so that the image windows cover the work area. If Automatically Tile mode is active when you close an image file or open a new one, Photoshop Elements will rearrange the image windows in tile formation.

Multi-window enables you to resize, arrange, or minimize files.

There are two ways to switch from one mode to another.

• Use the Window > Images menu and choose the arrangement you want: Maximize, Tile, or Cascade. Or, if there is a checkmark on the Maximize command, choosing Maximize again deactivates it and switches to Multi-window mode.

• Select an icon on the far right end of the menu bar.

The available icons vary, depending on which viewing mode is active and on the size of the work area on your monitor. If the work area is reduced, these icons may not appear. The illustration below shows which icons you'll see in different modes.

Icons available with Maximize mode active, Automatically Tile mode active, and Multi-window mode active.

For more information, see Adobe Photoshop Elements 4.0 Help.

Adjusting the results of an automatic fix

In this procedure, you'll experiment with one of the sliders in the Quick Fix palettes.

1   In the Photo Bin, select the 04_02 copy thumbnail to make it the active file.

2   Click the Auto button for Color. The results are the same as you had in the previous procedure.

3   Drag the Temperature slider a small amount to the left.

This cools down the image, enhancing the blue and green tones while reducing yellows, reds, and oranges.

4   Examine the results, paying particular attention to the skin tones and water colors.

5   Readjust the Temperature slider until you are satisfied with the realistic balance between warm skin tones and cool water colors. Then click the Commit button (✔) at the top of the Color palette. We moved our Temperature slider slightly to the left.

Note: If you aren't happy with the results and want to start over, click Cancel (⊘) on the Color palette tab. If you decide to undo the color fix after you click the Commit button, click the Reset button above the image. This restores the image to its original condition.

6   Choose File > Save, saving the file in the My CIB Work folder and in JPEG format, changing the name to **04_02 copy_Work**. Make sure Save in Version Set with Original is deselected. Click Save, leaving all other options in the Save and JPEG Options dialog boxes unchanged.

Combining automatic fix and manual image corrections

The top four commands in the Enhance menu apply the same changes as the Auto buttons in Quick Fix. These commands are available in both Quick Fix and Standard Edit.

Both Quick Fix and Standard Edit offer other methods of enhancing color in images. These are found on submenus on the lower half of the Enhance menu. In this procedure, you use a manual option to tweak the results produced by an automatic fix button.

1   In the Photo Bin, select the 04_02 copy 2 thumbnail to make it the active file.

2   In the Color palette, click Auto to apply the automatic color correction.

3   Choose Enhance > Adjust Color > Color Variations.

4   In the lower left area of the dialog box, make sure that Midtones is selected and that the Amount slider is approximately centered. Then, do the following:

•   Click the Increase Blue thumbnail once.

•   Click the Decrease Red thumbnail once, and click OK.

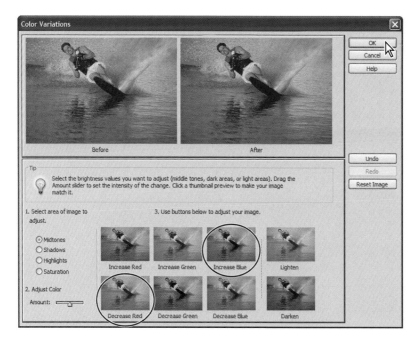

5 Choose File > Save As and navigate to the My CIB Work folder. Rename the file **04_ 02 copy 2_Work** and select the JPEG format. Deselect Save in Version Set with Original if it is selected. Click Save in the shortcuts bar, and accept the default JPEG Options.

This combination of fixes gives the water a turquoise look and makes the swimming trunks electric green. To try a different combination, you can undo the changes and start again. (Choose Edit > Undo Color Variations, and then try again, starting with Step 3.)

Comparing results

As you can tell by viewing the Photo Bin, all three copies of the image are open. You'll compare them to the file you processed at the beginning of this lesson.

1 Choose File > Open. Locate and select the My CIB Work folder. Select the Autofix_ 04_02 file and click Open.

2 Select Standard Edit (⬛) on the shortcuts bar to switch to that mode.

3 Choose Window > Images > Tile, if it's not already selected.

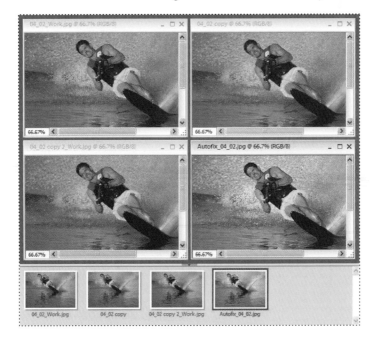

4 In the toolbox, select the Zoom tool (🔍).

5   In the tool options bar, select Zoom Out, and then do one of the following:

•   Click in the active image window until you can see the entire photo. Then choose Window > Images > Match Zoom.

•   If it's not already selected, select Zoom All Windows in the tool options bar, and then click in the active window.

Look for the highlighted thumbnail in the Photo Bin to see which file is active. Or look at the title bars of the open image windows; the text is dimmed on inactive image windows.

6   Examine the water, spray, skin tones, and clothing colors in the four versions. Decide which image looks best. Then drag any corner edge of the image window to resize it so it fills the space, and turn off automatic tiling.

7   Choose View > Fit on Screen to enlarge the image so it fits in the window.

Adjusting skin tones

Sometimes the combination of ambient light and surrounding color can cause skin tones in your image to be tinted with unwanted color. Photoshop Elements offers a unique solution, in both the Standard and Quick Fix modes.

To adjust color for skin tones:

1   Choose Enhance > Adjust Color > Adjust Color for Skin Tone.

2   Click on the waterskier's skin with the eyedropper cursor that appears.
Photoshop Elements automatically adjusts the entire photo to improve the color of the
waterskier's skin.

3   If you're unsatisfied with the correction, click on a different point in the image or
move the Tan, Blush, and Temperature sliders to achieve the desired result.

4   When you're satisfied with the skin tone, click OK and then choose File > Close All.
When asked, do not save the changes.

Working with red eye

Red eye occurs when a camera flash is reflected off the human retina so that the dark
center of the eye looks bright red. Photoshop Elements can automatically fix red eye
when you bring photos into the Organizer. Just select Automatically Fix Red Eyes in the
Get Photos dialog box when you import your photos.

Using automatic Red Eye Fix

Just as you automatically corrected color balance earlier in this lesson with Smart Fix,
you can also apply an automatic red eye correction in Quick Fix mode. This method
might not successfully remove red eye from all images, but Photoshop Elements
provides other options.

For this project, you'll use a flash photo of a boy and his dog, concentrating first on
removing the boy's red eyes.

1   Click the Photo Browser button to load the Organizer workspace. If you only see
one image, select the Back to All Photos button.

2   If necessary, in the Tags palette, click the Find box to the left of the Lesson 4 tag.

3   Open the file for this exercise by double-clicking on the uncorrected picture of the
boy and his dog, 04_03.jpg.

4   Click on the photo to select it, and choose Edit > Go to Quick Fix.

5   In the Palette Bin, under General Fixes, click the Auto button for Red Eye Fix. There is no slider available for this correction. As you can see, the Auto correction has no effect on this image.

The Red Eye Fix feature works for many images, but in this example extra steps are required.

Note: The Red Eye Fix correction is also available as a command under the Enhance menu, along with other automatic correction controls like Smart Fix, in both Quick Fix and Standard Edit modes.

The Red Eye Removal tool

For those stubborn red eye problems, the Red Eye Removal tool (⊹🍞) is a simple and automatic solution. In this part of the lesson, you will remove the red eye from the boy's eyes.

1   Have 04_03.jpg open in either Quick Fix or Standard Edit. If you choose to work in Standard Edit, work on the After version of the image.

2   Select the Zoom tool and click on the Zoom In button (🔍) in the tool options bar, then click and drag to surround the boy's eyes.

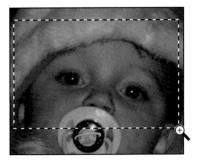

3   Select the Red Eye Removal tool (👁).

4   Click and release the mouse on the red area of the boy's left eye.

When you release the mouse button the red is removed from the eye.

You can also drag to create a selection with the Red Eye Removal tool.

5   Using the Red Eye Removal tool, click and drag to draw a selection surrounding the boy's right eye.

As smart as the Red Eye Removal tool is, its use is limited to red eyes. You can't use it to make your brown eyes blue. It also won't work for other colors of retinal reflections, such as the glowing eyes of an animal struck by a light beam or camera flash. Fortunately, there's another tool that does the job almost as easily as the Red Eye Removal tool.

Darkening reflective animal eyes

For this part of the lesson, you'll focus on the dog in the image. This picture is typical of the kind of retinal reflection that animal eyes produce in response to direct, strong light.

1   Make sure that the picture of the boy and his dog, 04_03.jpg, is still open. If you are not in Standard Edit mode, click the Standard Edit button now.

2   In the toolbox, do the following:

• Press **D** on your keyboard to set the colors to the default black and white. Or click the Default Foreground and Background Colors icon (■), located below the Foreground Color and Background Color swatches in the toolbox.

• Hold down the mouse on the Brush tool (✐) until the hidden tools appear. Select the Color Replacement tool (✌).

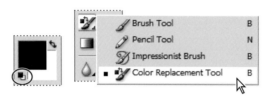

Notice that the tool options change.

3   Locate the Brush drop-down menu. Click and hold on the arrow to the right of the Brush size. If 13, the default, is not selected, use the slider or type **13** in the Diameter text field. Press Enter to close this menu.

Diameter:	13 px
Hardness:	100%
Spacing:	25%
Angle:	0°
Roundness:	100%
Size:	Pen Pressure
Tolerance:	Off

4   In the Mode drop-down menu, select Luminosity.

5   Select the Sampling: Once button (⊘).

About Sampling options for the Color Replacement tool

The Sampling option determines what colors will be changed by the Color Replacement tool. That color is determined by sampling the pixels that are directly under the crosshairs in the center of the brush shape. There are two types of sampling: Once and Continuous.

Once—Use this option to keep the sampling color the same throughout each stroke. For example, if the crosshairs are over a yellow area when you start to drag, then only yellow areas of the image will be changed as you continue the brush stroke across the image. If the crosshairs pass over a different color, the Color Replacement tool still changes only pixels matching the original yellow sample. This option is a good choice for changing small areas that don't have much variation in color, such as the dog's eyes.

Continuous—Use this option to constantly resample as you move the Color Replacement tool. For example, if the position of the crosshairs is over a yellow area when you start to drag, and then the crosshairs pass over a red area, the Color Replacement tool will start out changing yellow pixels and then begin changing red pixels. The Continuous sampling option works better for large areas with shifts of color because you can release the mouse button from time to time. In this way, if you make a mistake and want to undo a step, you won't lose all your color replacement work, just the most recent stroke.

6   Type **25** into the Tolerance text field, and press Enter.

💡 *For some tool options, you can change the value by scrubbing. To scrub, move the cursor over the label (such as the word Tolerance for the Color Replacement tool), so that the cursor changes to include a double-sided arrow (✥). Drag the cursor left or right across the label to make the number larger or smaller.*

If your Navigator palette is not visible, choose Window > Navigator.

7   In the Navigator palette, drag the slider to the right to enlarge your view. Then drag the red frame to the dog's face in the thumbnail so that the dog's left eye is centered in the image and fill most of the image window.

8	Center the Color Replacement tool over the upper part of the eye on the left side. Drag over the pupil without releasing until black fills most of the pupil area. One small surface highlight area remains white.

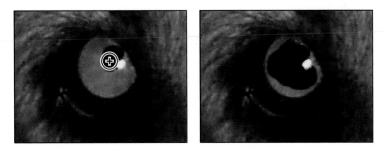

Note: If you keep the brush within the shape of the pupil, the tool will replace only the brilliant yellow color reflected by the dog's retina. If your results differ, review the tool options settings and try again.

9	Scroll to the right, so the eye on the right side is centered in the window. Move the crosshairs over the right eye and drag over that pupil to make it solid black.

Using the Navigator palette

The Navigator palette is an easy way to zoom and scroll in an image. The beauty of this feature is that you can remain on your current tool, and yet zoom in and out of your image. Dragging the red frame to the area you want to see is considerably quicker than doing vertical and horizontal scrolling. This method also helps you keep oriented about what part of the image you're seeing at very high zoom levels.

Restoring surface highlights

Unlike retinal reflections, surface reflections from the surface of the eye add realism and liveliness to a picture. The Color Replacement tool left the surface reflection in one of the dog's eyes. You'll take advantage of that by copying the reflection into the other eye.

1	In the toolbox, select the Elliptical Marquee tool (⬭), which is grouped with the Rectangular Marquee tool (⬚).

2 Scroll back to the left eye. Drag a selection marquee around the small, white reflection in the eye on the left, including some of the black area.

3 If necessary, zoom in even more so that the eye is very large. (200% works well for this step.) Then select the Move tool (▶⊕).

4 Position the cursor inside the selection. The cursor then appears as a black arrowhead (▶).

5 Clone or copy the selected area by holding down the Alt key and dragging a short distance. Release the Alt key and drag the copied selection into the dog's other eye.

Note: Be careful not to drag one of the corner handles; this would enlarge and distort the selection instead of moving it. If that happens, click Cancel (⊘) in the tool options bar and try again.

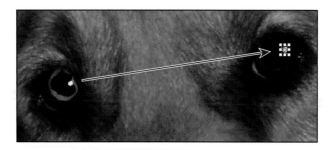

6 Deselect the selection by choosing Select > Deselect.

7 Drag the slider in the Navigator palette to the left until you can see the entire image, and review the overall results.

8 Choose File > Save As. Navigate to the My CIB Work folder and name the file **04_ 03_Work**. Select the JPEG format. Keep Save in Version Set with Original deselected. Then click Save. Click OK in the JPEG Options dialog box.

9 Choose File > Close to close the 04_03_Work.jpg file.

Holding down the Alt key while you drag with the Move tool is a power-user technique. It's almost the same as copying and pasting, except that copying and pasting places the copied area onto a separate layer. As you can see in the Layers palette, Alt+dragging leaves the copied pixels on the same layer as its source.

Congratulations. You've learned how to use the Color Replacement tool for situations where the Red Eye Removal tool doesn't produce results. You've also learned a nifty shortcut for duplicating the image in a selected area by Alt+dragging with the Move tool. In the next exercise, you'll learn about the many ways you can use selections to control where adjustments occur within an image.

Making selections

In the previous exercise you were introduced to the process of creating selections by using the elliptical marquee. Ordinarily, the entire image area can be altered by the changes you apply to an image or image layer. That's because, as a default, the whole image is active. A selection is a portion of the image area that you designate as the only active area of the image. When a selection is active, any changes you apply affect only the area within the selection; the rest of the image layer is protected, or masked.

Typically, a selection marquee—a border of dashed black and white lines that flashes—shows the boundaries of a selection. You can save a selection and re-use it at a later time. This can be a terrific time-saver when you need to use the selection several times.

Several tools create selections, and you'll get experience with most of them in the course of doing the lessons in this book. Selections can be geometric in shape or free form, and they can have crisp or soft edges. Selections can be created by using the mouse, or by using similarities of color within the image.

Perhaps the simplest, most effective way to create a selection is to paint it on an image. This exercise focuses on the use of two selection tools in Photoshop Elements, the Selection Brush and the Magic Selection Brush.

1 Using the Organizer, select the image of the flower, 04_04.psd. Then switch to Standard Edit mode by choosing Edit > Go to Standard Edit.

2 Though it is not visible, a portion of the flower has already been selected and saved in the file. You'll now make your own selection and add it to the saved selection.

3 In the toolbox, select the Selection Brush tool ( ). It is grouped with the Magic Selection Brush tool.

Using the Selection Brush tool

The Selection Brush tool makes selections in two ways. You can paint over the area you want to select in Selection mode, or you can paint over areas you don't want to select using a semi-opaque overlay in Mask mode.

1 From the options bar, set the Selection Brush controls to the following:

- Add to selection
- 25 pixels wide
- Mode: Selection
- Hardness: 100%

2   Click and drag with the Selection Brush to paint over the large interior areas of the top two petals of the flower. Do not try to paint the edges, you will do that in the next step.

Notice that as you paint, you're actually painting with the flashing dashed line that indicates a selection. Release the mouse button to see what you've selected.

Now you'll reduce your brush size and paint the edges of the two petals, adding them to your selection as you paint.

While you could move the Size slider to change your brush size, it's easier to use the open bracket key ([ ) to size the brush down, and the close bracket key ( ]) to size the brush up. The brush size increases or decreases in size each time you press the open or close bracket key.

3   Press the left bracket key ([ ), to reduce the Selection Brush size to 10 pixels.

4   Paint the edges of the two top petals with the Selection Brush by clicking and dragging over them.

5   Continue to paint, using the brackets to change the brush size as needed, until the top two petals have a selection outline completely encompassing them.

Editing a saved selection

Next you'll add your selection to the pre-made selection, which was saved with the file. For more information on saving selections, see "Changing the color of a pictured object" later in this lesson. You can modify saved selections by replacing, adding to, or subtracting from them.

1   With your selection still active, choose Select > Load Selection.

2   In the Load Selection dialog box, choose low_petals and in the Operation section, choose Add to Selection. Click OK.

Note: The New Selection option replaces the saved selection with the current selection. Subtract from Selection subtracts the current selection from the saved selection. Intersect with Selection replaces the saved selection with the intersection between the current selection and the saved selection.

3   You should now see the entire flower outlined by the flashing selection boundary.

If you've missed a spot, simply paint it in with the Selection Brush tool. If you've selected too much, click on the Subtract from Selection button in the shortcuts bar and "paint out" your mistakes.

Note: You can also modify a saved selection by loading it and using selection tools to add to it (Shift+drag) or subtract from it (Alt+drag).

By switching the Mode in the options bar from Selection to Mask, you can use the Selection Brush to paint out the areas that you don't want selected in your image.

Leave the flower selected.

Using the Magic Selection Brush

The Magic Selection Brush works similarly to the Selection Brush, except that it allows you to draw, scribble, or click on the object you want to be selected (or in this case, masked). The mark you make doesn't need to be precise, because when you release the mouse, Photoshop Elements draws the selection border.

1 In the Toolbox, select the Magic Selection Brush tool (✐).

If the Adobe Photoshop Elements window appears, click OK.

2 In the options bar, make sure New Selection is selected.

3 In the options bar, choose a brush size from the Size menu. If you want to simply scribble over the area, you can use a larger brush. For a more precise outline, choose a smaller brush size.

4   In the flower image's background, do one of the following to create a selection:

•   Click on an area in the background.

•   Click and drag to draw a selection around the area behind the flower.

•   Scribble over the background, and then release the mouse button.

The tool draws red on your image, but turns into a selection when you release the mouse. Now that the background is selected, you will turn the selection "inside out."

5   Turn the selection inside out, thereby masking the background and selecting the flower, by choosing Select > Inverse.

To tighten up the selection, you can choose, from the tool options, the Indicate Foreground tool (✎) to add to the selection, or the Indicate Background tool (✎) to subtract from the selection.

The value of selections

You now have a flashing selection outline around the flower. You'll now apply a simple hue adjustment in Quick Fix mode.

1   With the flower image open, click on the Quick Fix button in the shortcuts toolbar to launch that mode.

2   To make comparing easier, choose Before and After (Portrait) from the View drop-down in the lower left.

3   From the Color Auto Fix palette on the right, click and drag the Hue slider to the right to change the color of the flower.

Notice that the flower changes color, but the leafy background does not. This is because only pixels inside the selection change.

4   Choose File > Close, without saving your changes.

Congratulations, you've finished another exercise. In this exercise, you've learned how to use the Selection Brush and the Magic Selection Brush to isolate areas of an image. You've also learned to mask out areas that you don't want changes to be applied to. And you've learned how to add these new selections to existing, saved selections. This knowledge will be invaluable as you learn to use other selection tools.

Changing the color of a pictured object

Photoshop Elements offers two methods of swapping color. The first method is to use the Color Replacement tool, as you did when you replaced yellow with black in the dog's eyes. You can also use this technique to change any color simply by changing the Foreground Color.

The second method is to use the Replace Color window. It's faster and more automatic than using the Color Replacement tool, but it doesn't work well for all types of images. This method is easiest when the color of the object you want to change is not found in other areas of the image. The color photograph of a bright yellow truck has very little yellow elsewhere in the image, making it a perfect example for this approach.

You will use the Replace Color window in the next exercise.

Setting up layers and saving a selection

In this project, you'll change the color of a yellow truck. You'll do your work on a duplicate of the Background layer, which makes it easy to compare the finished project with the original picture.

In a previous exercise, you made a selection of the highlight in the dog's eye. In this project, you're going to make a more difficult, free-form selection. As a safeguard, you're going to save the selection shape itself as a permanent part of the work file. Saving any complex selection is a good idea if there's any chance you may have to use it again, either to retrace your steps or to do something else with that selection.

1 Using the Organizer, find the 04_05.jpg file, the picture of the yellow truck. Open it in Standard Edit mode by choosing Edit > Go to Standard Edit.

2 Choose Layer > Duplicate Layer and accept the default name, or drag the Background layer up to the New Layer icon (▣) in the Layers palette. By duplicating the layer, you have an original to return to if you need it.

3 Select the Lasso tool (♀) and click and drag with the mouse to draw a rough selection around the truck. It's OK if some of the road and background shrubbery are included in the selection.

Note: The Lasso tool is found in the toolbox with the Magnetic Lasso tool (♥) and the Polygonal Lasso tool (♥). You can quickly switch from one lasso tool to another by selecting it in the tool options bar instead of using the drop-down in the toolbox.

4 In the tool options bar, select Subtract from Selection (🖫), and then drag a shape around some of the background greenery to remove it from the selection.

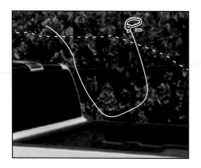

Note: It may be helpful to zoom in for this part of the process. Use the slider in the Navigator palette to zoom in so that you don't have to switch tools, or use the zoom-in keyboard shortcut, Ctrl+ = (equal sign).

5 Continue to remove areas of greenery from the selection until the selection marquee fits reasonably well around the top of the truck—it doesn't need to be perfect, as long as the entire truck is included.

6 Choose Select > Save Selection, and name the selection **Truck**. Click OK.

7   Press Ctrl+D to deselect, or choose Select > Deselect.

If you zoomed in for Step 4, you can zoom out by clicking Ctrl+O so that you can see the whole image.

Replacing a color throughout the image

What's nice about the Replace Color feature is that you don't have to be too careful when you apply it. In spite of that, you can produce spectacular results. You're going to do this exercise twice. First you'll do it without loading the selection you saved. This will show you how much the color changes will affect the areas outside the truck, such as the landscaping. You will then use your saved selection for the second part of this exercise.

1   In the Layers palette, select the Background Copy layer, if it is not already selected.

2   Choose Enhance > Adjust Color > Replace Color.

3   In the Replace Color dialog box, select Image so that you see the color thumbnail of the truck picture, and make sure that the Eyedropper tool (🖋) within the dialog box is selected. Then click a bright area of the yellow paint.

4   Click the Selection option under the thumbnail to see a black-and-white thumbnail, where white indicates the area that is selected.

5   Drag the Hue, Saturation, and Lightness sliders to change the color of the selected area. For example, try Hue = –60, Saturation = 8, and Lightness = –9 to make the truck red.

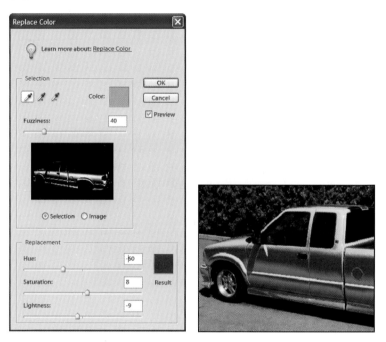

6   To adjust the color-application area, start by selecting the Add to Sample eyedropper ( ), and click the thumbnail in an area corresponding to paint that still has a mustardy tinge to it.

7 Drag the Fuzziness slider to the right until you reach an acceptable compromise between the color replacement on the truck and the effect the change has on the bushes in the background.

8 When you are satisfied with the results, click OK.

Depending on what color and color characteristics you used to replace the yellow, you probably can see a shift in the color of the shrubbery behind the truck. If this is a compromise you can live with, that's great. If not, you may need to try another technique, which is what you'll do in the next procedure.

Replacing a color in a limited area of the image

You're going to try the previous procedure again, but this time you'll limit the affected area by loading a selection.

1 Choose Edit > Undo Replace Color, or select the step before Replace Color on the Undo History palette.

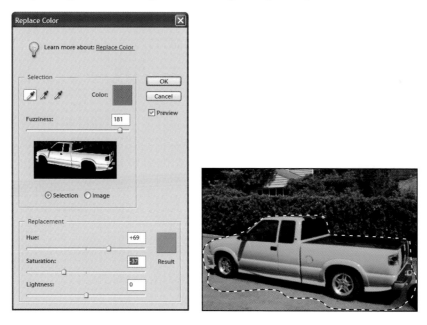

2 Choose Select > Load Selection. Make sure that Truck is displayed as the selection, and click OK.

3 Choose Enhance > Adjust Color > Replace Color.

4 Using the same techniques and settings you used in the previous procedure, make adjustments in the Replace Color dialog box to change the color of the truck. (See "Replacing a color throughout the image," steps 3-6.)

5   When you are satisfied with the results, click OK to close the dialog box.

6   Choose Select > Deselect, or press Ctrl+D.

7   Choose File > Save As, and save the file in the My CIB Work folder. For File Name, type **04_05_Work**. Make sure that the Format option is Photoshop (PSD). If Save in Version Set with Original is selected, deselect it before you click Save.

8   Choose File > Close, to close the file.

Take a bow—you've finished the five exercises in this lesson. In the last exercise, you learned how to make a selection with the Lasso tool. You edited that selection to make it fit more closely, and you saved it so that you can reload it on the image later or in future work sessions. You then replaced one color with another using the Replace Color dialog box rather than the Color Replacement brush. In the process, you've also used the Undo History palette to step backwards to a specific point in your work.

Saving and organizing finished files

You'll use tags to organize the new work files. These lesson files offer an opportunity to use the Stacking feature in the Organizer, which makes reviewing and finding image files even easier.

1   If necessary, click Photo Browser ( ) on the shortcuts bar to switch to the Organizer. If the Back to All Photos button appears on the Organizer shortcuts bar, select it.

2   Drag the Work Files tag to the thumbnails to apply it to the work files you created in this lesson.

3 Select the first waterskier thumbnail and then hold down Ctrl and click each of the waterskier thumbnails. The waterskier thumbnails are highlighted with a blue outline.

4 Choose Edit > Stack > Stack Selected Photos.

Now only one waterskier image appears, but it has a Stack icon in the upper right corner, indicating that other versions of this image are stacked with it.

5 Repeat Steps 4 and 5 for all copies of the dog, the vases, and the truck.

You can change which image appears at the top of a stack by selecting the stack thumbnail and choosing Edit > Stack > Reveal Photos in Stack. This limits the Organizer thumbnail display to just the images in that stack. Select the thumbnail you want to use, and choose Edit > Stack > Set As Top Photo. When you click Back to All Photos above the thumbnail area, the thumbnail you selected appears at the top.

Why won't Photoshop Elements do what I tell it to do?

In some situations, the changes you try to apply to an image may not seem to work. Or you may hear a beep sound, indicating that you're trying to do something that's not allowed.

The following list offers common explanations and solutions for what might be blocking your progress.

Commit is required

Several tools, including the Type tool (**T**) require you to click the Commit button (✔) in the tool options bar before you can move on to another task. The same is true when you crop with the Crop tool or resize a layer or selection with the Move tool.

Cancel is required

The Undo command isn't available while you have uncommitted changes made with the Type tool, Move tool, or Crop tool, for example. If you want to undo those changes, click Cancel (⊘) in the tool options bar instead of using the Undo command or shortcut.

Edits are restricted by an active selection

When you create a selection (using a marquee tool, the Magic Wand tool, or the Selection Brush tool, for example), you limit the active area of the image. Any edits you make will apply only within the selected area. If you try to make changes to an area outside the selection, nothing happens. If you want to deactivate a selection, choose Select > Deselect, and then you can work on any area of the image.

Move tool is required

If you drag a selection, the selection marquee, not the image within the selection marquee, moves. If you want to move a selected part of the image or an entire layer, use the Move tool (▸₊).

Background layer is selected

Many changes cannot be applied to the Background layer. For example, you can't erase, delete, change the opacity, or drag the Background layer to a higher level in the layer stack. If you need to apply changes to the Background layer, double-click it and rename it (or accept the default name, Layer 0).

(*continued*)

Why won't Photoshop Elements do what I tell it to do? *(cont'd)*

Active layer is hidden

In most cases, the edits you make apply to only the currently selected layer—the one highlighted in the Layers palette. If an eye icon (👁) does not appear by that layer in the Layers palette, then the layer is hidden and you cannot edit it. Or, if the image on the selected layer is not visible because it is blocked by an opaque upper layer, you actually will be changing that layer but you won't see the changes in the image window.

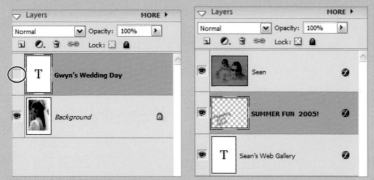

The active layer is hidden, and layer view blocked by opaque upper layer.

Active layer is locked

If you lock a layer by selecting the layer and then selecting the Lock (🔒) in the Layers palette, the lock prevents the layer from changing. To unlock a layer, select the layer and then select the Lock at the top of the Layers palette to remove the lock.

Locking or unlocking a layer.

Wrong layer is selected (for editing text)

If you want to make changes to a text layer, be sure that layer is selected in the Layers palette before you start. If a nontext layer is selected when you click the Type tool in the image window, Photoshop Elements creates a new text layer instead of placing the cursor in the existing text layer.

About printing color pictures

Sometimes, pictures that look great on your computer don't turn out so well when you print them. How can you make them look as good in print as they do on screen?

Color problems can arise from a variety of sources. One may be the camera or the conditions under which the photograph was taken. If the photograph is flawed, then you can usually make it better by editing it with Photoshop Elements, as you did with the images in this lesson.

There are other possible contributors to color problems. One may be your monitor, which may shift colors. You can correct that by calibrating your monitor.

Another possibility is that your color printer interprets color information differently than your computer. You can correct that by activating the appropriate type of color management.

Working with color management

Moving an image from your camera to your monitor, and finally to a printer, makes the image colors shift. This shift occurs because every device has a different color gamut, or range of colors, that it can display or produce. To achieve consistent color among digital cameras, scanners, computer monitors, and printers, you need to use color management.

Color management acts as a color interpreter, translating the image colors so that each device can reproduce them in the same way. It knows how each device and/or program understands color, and adjusts colors so that the colors you see on your monitor are similar to the colors in your printed image. It should be noted, however, that not all colors may match exactly.

Color management is achieved through the use of profiles, or mathematical descriptions of each device's color space. If these profiles are compliant with the standards of the ICC (International Color Consortium), they help you maintain consistent color.

Photoshop Elements' color management controls are located under the Edit menu.

Setting up color management

1   In the Editor, choose Edit > Color Settings.

2   Select one of these color management options:

•   **No Color Management** uses your monitor profile as the working space. It removes any embedded profiles when opening images, and does not tag or apply a profile when saving.

•   **Always Optimize for Computer Screens** uses sRGB as the working space, preserves embedded profiles, and assigns sRGB when opening untagged files.

•   **Always Optimize for Printing** uses Adobe RGB as the working space, preserves embedded profiles, and assigns Adobe RGB when opening untagged files.

•   **Allow Me to Choose** lets you choose to assign sRGB (the default) or Adobe RGB when opening untagged files.

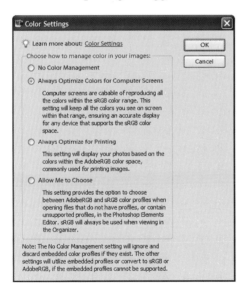

3   Click OK.

Note: *When you save a file, select ICC Profile in the Save As dialog box.*

Further information on color management, including monitor calibration, can be found in a series of topics in Help. To access this information, choose Help > Photoshop Elements Help and search for these subjects.

Review

▶ **Review questions**

1   What is the key difference between adjusting an image in Standard Edit mode versus adjusting it in Quick Fix mode?

2   Can you apply automatic fixes when you are in Standard Edit mode?

3   What tool do you use to manually fix the red-eye phenomenon created by some flash cameras? Can you use the same tool to fix glowing animal eyes?

4   What makes selections so important for adjusting color?

5   Name two selection tools and describe how they work.

▶ **Review answers**

1   Standard Edit provides a more flexible and powerful image correction environment. It has lighting and color correction commands, along with tools you'll need to fix image defects, make selections, add text, and paint on your images. Quick Fix provides access to the more basic photo fixing controls in Photoshop Elements, and allows you to make quick adjustments to your images using those controls.

2   Yes. The Enhance menu contains commands that are equivalent to the buttons in the Quick Fix palettes: Auto Smart Fix, Auto Levels, Auto Contrast, Auto Color Correction, and Auto Red Eye Fix. The Enhance menu also provides an Adjust Smart Fix command, which opens a dialog box in which you can change the amount of automatic fixing.

3   The Red Eye Removal tool does an extraordinarily good job of automatically fixing red eye. However, it works only with red, not with the glowing yellow or green eyes that a camera flash or other strong light will create in an animal's eyes. To change animal eyes, you need to use other techniques, such as using the Color Replacement tool, as described in this lesson.

4   You use a selection to define an area as the only part of a layer that can be altered. The areas outside the selection are protected from change for as long as the selection is active. This aids greatly in image correction, as it allows you make different adjustments to selected portions of your image.

5   The Elliptical Marquee tool and the Rectangular Marquee tool make selections in fixed geometric shapes when you drag them across the image. Another tool you can use to make selections is the Selection Brush tool, which works like a paintbrush. Similar to the Selection Brush, the Magic Selection Brush tool is a faster, more flexible option for creating a selection. The Lasso tool creates free-form selections; you drag the Lasso tool around the area that you want to select. You can also use the Magic Wand tool, which selects all the areas with the same color as the color on which you click.

5 | Fixing Exposure Problems

You can use Photoshop Elements to fix most images that are too dark or too light. This lesson leads you through several approaches to correcting exposure problems in photographs. This aspect of color correction is often easier to fix than you might imagine.

In this lesson you will learn how to do the following:

• Brighten underexposed photographs.

• Bring out details and colors in overexposed and faded photographs.

• Correct different areas of an image individually.

• Save selection shapes to reuse in later sessions.

• Create and apply adjustment layers.

Most users can complete this lesson in a little over an hour.

This lesson assumes that you are already familiar with the overall features of the Photoshop Elements 4.0 work area and recognize the two ways in which you can use Photoshop Elements: the Editor and the Organizer. If you need to learn more about these items, see Lesson 1, "A Quick Tour of Photoshop Elements" and Photoshop Elements Help. This lesson also builds on the skills and concepts covered in the earlier lessons.

If you are starting your work in this book with this lesson, make sure that you have already copied the project files from the CD attached to the inside back cover of this book. See "Copying the Classroom in a Book files" on page 3.

In this lesson, you will use the CIB Catalog you created earlier in the book. If necessary, open this catalog by choosing File > Catalog in Photo Organizer, then click Open

Getting started

You'll start this lesson in the same way as you started your work in Lesson 4. You will process all the image files for this lesson at once to apply automatic fixes available in Photoshop Elements 4.0. You'll save these files so that you can compare them to the files that you fix using manual techniques.

1   Start Photoshop Elements in Standard Edit by selecting Edit and Enhance Photos on the Welcome Screen. Or, if the Organizer is open, click Edit (🔧) and choose Go to Standard Edit.

2   Choose File > Process Multiple Files.

3   In the Process Multiple Files window, do the following:

• Choose Folder on the Process Files From drop-down menu.

• Under Source, select the Browse button, and then locate and select the Lesson05 folder, and click OK.

• Under Destination, click Browse, and then locate and select the My CIB Work folder.

• Select Rename Files. Type **Autofix_** in the first option, and select Document Name in the second option. This adds the prefix "Autofix_" to the existing document name as the files are saved in the My CIB Work folder.

4   On the right side of the window, select all four Quick Fix options: Auto Levels, Auto Contrast, Auto Color, and Sharpen. Review your settings, and then click OK.

It takes a few seconds for Photoshop Elements to process the files. Image windows will open and close automatically as the changes are applied. There's nothing else you need to do. If any alerts or warnings are displayed, click OK.

At the end of this lesson, you'll compare the results of this simple, automatic fixing of the images with the manual techniques. In many cases, this automatic method of fixing files may be sufficient to meet your needs.

Brightening an underexposed image

Slightly underexposed photographs look dingy and dull. While the auto-fix lighting feature does a terrific job of brightening up many of these photos, here you'll use layers to adjust the exposure.

Note: You'll need to access the files in the CIB Catalog you created at the start of this book. If this catalog is not open, open it now by choosing File > Catalog and clicking Open.

1   Click the Photo Browser button to load the Organizer workspace.

2   In the Tags palette, click the Find box to the left of the Lesson 5 tag.

3   Open the file for this exercise by double-clicking the picture of the girl in the kitchen.

4   Choose Go to Standard Edit from the Edit menu in the shortcuts bar.

5   Do only one of the following to duplicate the Background layer of the image:

•   Choose Layer > Duplicate Layer, and click OK to accept the default name.

•   Right-click Background in the Layers palette, and choose Duplicate Layer. Click OK.

•   Drag the Background to the New Layer shortcut (▣) at the top of the Layers palette.

The new Background Copy layer is highlighted in the Layers palette, indicating it is the selected (active) layer.

6 In the Layers palette, choose Screen as the blending mode. Notice how the image becomes brighter.

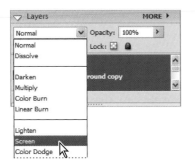

Note: If the drop-down menu shown above is not available, make sure that the Background Copy layer, not the original Background layer, is selected in the Layers palette.

7 Choose File > Save, and save the file as 05_01_Work.psd in the My CIB Work folder that you created at the start of the book. Make sure that Include in the Organizer is selected, and that you've deselected the Save in Version Set with the Original option.

If a message appears about maximizing compatibility, click OK to close it. Or, follow the instructions in the message to prevent it from appearing again.

8 When you've finished viewing the results, close the file.

Here you've seen how simple it is to use blending modes to brighten a dull image. In other exercises, you'll use other blending modes to correct different kinds of image problems.

Improving faded or overexposed images

In this exercise, you'll work with the scan of an old photograph that has faded badly and is in danger of being lost forever. Although it's not necessarily an award-winning shot, it could represent an era of personal history that you might want to preserve for future generations.

The automatic fixes you applied earlier in this lesson to a copy of this image improve the photograph quite a bit. In this project, you'll try to do even better using other techniques.

Creating a set of duplicate files

You're going to compare a variety of techniques during the course of this project. You'll start by creating individual files for each technique and giving them unique names. These names will help you identify the technique used to adjust each file.

1   If necessary, click on the Photo Browser button to load the Organizer workspace, then click the Back to All Photos button. Click the Find button for the Lesson 5 tag. Select the faded picture of the boy, then choose Edit > Go to Standard Edit from the shortcuts bar.

2   Choose File > Duplicate, and type **Shad_High** in the Duplicate Image dialog box, then click OK.

3   Repeat Step 2 two more times, naming the duplicate files **Bright_Con** and **Levels**.

4   In the Photo Bin, select the 05_02.jpg thumbnail to make that image active.

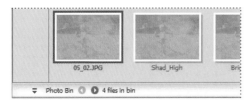

5   Choose File > Save As. When a dialog box appears, type **Blend_Mode** as the new file name and select Photoshop (PSD) in the Format drop-down menu. Select the My CIB Work folder as the Save In location. If Save in Version Set with Original is selected, be sure to deselect it before you click Save. Click OK in any dialog boxes or messages that appear to accept the default settings. Leave all four images open for the rest of the project.

Using blending modes to fix a faded image

This technique is similar to the one you used earlier to correct an underexposed image. In this case, you'll use other blending modes to fix the exposure.

Blending modes make layers interact with the layers under them in various ways. Multiply intensifies the dark pixels in an image. Overlay tends to brighten an image. For this project, using Overlay adds clarity and brilliance without canceling out the effect of the Multiply blending mode on the underlying layers.

The stacking order of the layers makes a difference, so if you dragged one of the Multiply blending-mode layers to the top of the layer stack, you'd see slightly different results.

1 In the Photo Bin, make sure that Blend_Mode.psd is highlighted, or click its thumbnail to make it active.

2 Duplicate the Background layer (by choosing Layer > Duplicate Layer). Click OK in the dialog box that appears, to accept the default name, Background copy.
Leave the Background copy layer selected for the next step.

3 In the Layers palette, do both the following:

• Choose Multiply on the blending modes drop-down menu.

• Drag the Background copy layer to the New Layer icon (□) to create another duplicate, Background copy 2.

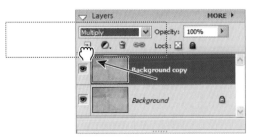

4   In the Layers palette, select the following options for the Background copy 2 layer:

• Change the blending mode from Multiply to Overlay.

• Set the Opacity to 50%, either by typing or by dragging the Opacity slider.

The Overlay blending mode brightens the image considerably, but the image contrast is still unimpressive.

5   Select the Background copy layer (not Background copy 2), and choose Layer > Duplicate Layer. Click OK in the dialog box to accept the default name, Background copy 3.

The new duplicate layer also has Multiply blending mode, which adds the extra bit of muscle this picture needs.

6   (Optional) Fine-tune the results by adjusting the Opacity settings for the individual layers until the image achieves a pleasing balance.

Note: You cannot change the Opacity of the locked Background layer.

7   Choose File > Save As, and save the file in the My CIB Work folder. If Save in Version Set with Original is selected, be sure to deselect it before you click Save. Choose to replace the existing file when asked. Leave the file open.

If a message appears about maximizing compatibility, click OK to close it. Or, follow the instructions in the message to prevent it from appearing again.

Adjusting shadows and highlights manually

Although both auto-fixing and blending modes do a good job of correcting fading images, some of your own photos may be more challenging. You'll try three new techniques in the next three procedures.

The first technique involves making adjustments for Shadows, Highlights, and Midtone Contrast.

1	In the Photo Bin, select the Shad_High thumbnail.

2	Choose Enhance > Adjust Lighting > Shadows/Highlights.

3	Select the Preview option in the Shadows/Highlights dialog box, if it is not already selected. If necessary, move the dialog box so that you can also see most of the Shad_ High image window.

By default, the Lighten Shadows setting is 25%, so you'll see a difference in the image already.

4	In the Shadows/Highlights dialog box, do all the following:

- Drag the Lighten Shadows slider to the right to 30%, or type **30**%.

- Drag the slider, or type, to set Darken Highlights at 15%.

- Drag the slider, or type, to set the Midtone Contrast at about +30%.

5	Readjust the three settings as needed until you think the image is as good as it can be. Then click OK to close the Shadows/Highlights dialog box.

6   Choose File > Save As, and save the file in the My CIB Work folder. If Save in Version Set with Original is selected, be sure to deselect it before you click Save. Click OK to accept the default settings in the JPEG Options dialog box. Leave the file open.

The adjustments you used in this technique are also available in the Lighting palette in Quick Fix mode.

Adjusting brightness and contrast manually

The next approach you'll take for fixing exposure problems uses another dialog box, which you open from the Enhance > Adjust Lighting menu.

1   In the Photo Bin, select the Bright_Con thumbnail.

2   Choose Enhance > Adjust Lighting > Brightness/Contrast.

If necessary, drag the window aside so that you can also see most of the Bright_Con image window.

3   In the Brightness/Contrast window, do all the following:

• Select Preview, if it is not already selected.

• Drag the Brightness slider to -30, or type **-30** in the box, being careful to include the minus sign when you type.

• Drag or type to set the Contrast at +55.

4   If necessary, adjust the Brightness and Contrast settings until you are happy with the quality of the image. Click OK to close the dialog box.

5   Choose File > Save As, and save the file in the My CIB Work folder as the location. If Save in Version Set with Original is selected, be sure to deselect it before you click Save. Click OK when the JPEG Options dialog box appears. Leave the file open.

Adjusting levels

Levels are the range of color values—the degree of darkness or lightness, whether the color is red, yellow, purple, or another color. In this procedure, you'll enhance the photograph by shifting the reference points for levels.

1   In the Photo Bin, select the Levels thumbnail.

2   Choose Enhance > Adjust Lighting > Levels.

3   Select the Preview option in the Levels dialog box, if it is not already selected.

The graph represents the distribution of pixel values in the image. There are no truly white pixels or truly black ones. By dragging the sliders inward to where the pixels start to appear in the graph, you redefine what levels are calculated as dark and light. This enhances the contrast between the lightest pixels in the image and the darkest ones.

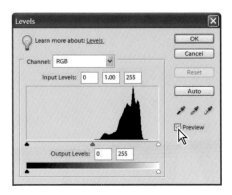

If necessary, drag the dialog box aside so that you can also see most of the image window.

4 In the Levels dialog box, do all the following:

• Drag the black arrow that is beneath the left side of the graph to the right and position it under the first steep spike in the graph shape. At that position, the value in the first Input Levels box is approximately 143.

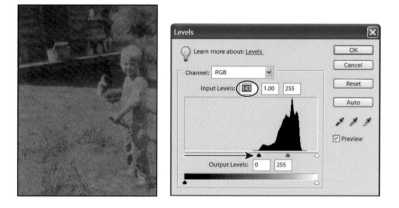

• Drag the white arrow on the right side of the graph until it reaches the edge of the final spike in the graph shape. The value of the third Input Levels box changes to approximately 225.

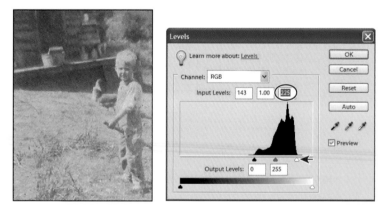

- Drag the gray center arrow under the graph toward the right until the middle Input Level value is approximately 0.90. Click OK to close the Levels dialog box.

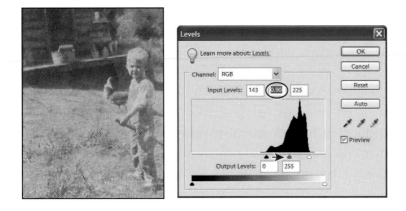

5   Choose File > Save As, and save it with the others in the My CIB Work folder. If Save in Version Set with Original is selected, be sure to deselect it before you click Save. Leave the file open after you click OK in the JPEG Options dialog box.

Comparing results

You can now compare the five versions of the image: these four and the one that you auto-fixed at the beginning of this lesson.

1   In Standard Edit, use the File > Open command to find and open the Autofix_05_02.jpg file in the My CIB Work folder.

2   In the Photo Bin, make sure that only the five files for this project are open: Blend_Mode, Shad_High, Bright_Con, Levels, and Autofix_05_02. Close any other open files.

3 Click Automatically Tile Windows on the right side of the menu bar or choose Window > Images > Tile.

Note: *If you do not see the icon for tiling windows, make sure that you are in Standard Edit mode, not Quick Fix.*

4 You'll reduce the zoom level for all active windows. Select the Zoom tool (🔍). In the tool options bar, select Zoom Out and Zoom All Windows. Then click in the image window until you can see the entire image.

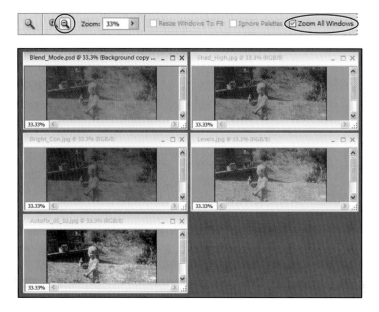

5 Compare the files. The best method for fixing a file depends on the type of problem being addressed, the affected areas of the image, and how you will use the resulting image.

6 Click Automatically Tile Windows (⊞) again to deselect it. You won't see any difference in the arrangement of image windows, but it will stop the automatic rearrangement when you open or close other images.

7 Choose File > Close All. Save your changes if prompted to do so.

Congratulations—you've successfully completed another exercise. In doing so, you've used various automatic and manual approaches to correct overexposed photographs and scans of faded prints. You've tried auto fixes, blending modes, and the three dialog boxes that are available on the Enhance > Adjust Lighting submenu. You know that you can apply these different adjustments either separately or in combinations.

Using adjustment layers to edit images

If you were to open one of the files from the previous exercise that used the Adjust Lighting submenu, you'd see that the values you entered when adjusting the images no longer appear. This change took place as soon as you clicked OK in those dialog boxes, before you closed the file. Because of this, it is not possible to return the Levels or other adjustments back to their starting point.

Sometimes you need to go back and tweak your settings after the first adjustment, or even during a much later work session. Adjustment layers are a way of applying changes to layers that you can easily revise.

Creating adjustment layers for lighting

In this project, you'll use a badly underexposed photograph of some flowering plants. It's hard to imagine that this picture could ever be useful, but Photoshop Elements can rescue what you perceive to be a hopelessly bad picture.

Before you begin, make sure that Photoshop Elements is open in Standard Edit mode and that the Layers palette is available in the Palette Bin.

1 Switch to the Organizer, then click the 05_03.jpg image, the picture of flowers, to select it. Choose Go to Standard Edit in the shortcuts bar to open the image in Standard Edit mode.

2 Click Create Adjustment Layer (◐.) on the Layers palette and choose Brightness/ Contrast from the drop-down menu.

3   If necessary, drag the Brightness/Contrast window aside so that you can also see most of the image window. In the Brightness/Contrast window, drag the sliders so that Brightness is +60 and Contrast is +30, then click OK.

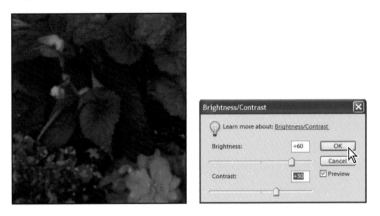

4   Repeat Step 2, but this time choose Levels (instead of Brightness/Contrast), so that the new adjustment layer will allow you to adjust levels.

5   In the Levels dialog box, drag the black, white, and gray arrows that are under the graph to the left or right until the balance of dark and light areas looks right to you. We selected values of 30, 1.2, and 155.

6   Click OK to close the Levels dialog box.

The beauty of adjustment layers is that you can revert to earlier settings, even in later work sessions, as long as you save the file in Photoshop (PSD) format (the default). For example, if you double-click the Brightness/Contrast icon in the layer thumbnail, your original settings (+60 and +30) still appear in the Brightness/Contrast dialog box, and can be further refined or removed.

If necessary, you can even revert to the original, uncorrected image by either hiding or deleting the adjustment layers. This is not necessary for this image. Keep the image open for the next exercise.

Applying an adjustment layer to a limited area

Although the adjustment layers do a fine job of bringing out the colors and details from the dark original image, the orange-colored blossoms are now too vivid. You'll compensate for this by adding a new adjustment layer that addresses color rather than lighting.

1   In the toolbox, select the Magic Wand tool (✳). In the tool options bar, type **48** for Tolerance, and make sure that New Selection and Contiguous are selected.

Tolerance: 48   ☑ Anti-alias ☑ Contiguous ☐ Sample All Layers

2   Click one of the two extremely bright blossoms in the upper area of the image. A selection marquee appears around most of the flower.

The selected blossom.

3   In the tool options bar, select Add to Selection (⬚).

4   Click the second bright blossom to add it to the selection. If necessary, click again to add any unselected patches of color within the two blossom areas.

Adding to the existing selection.

5   Choose Layer > New Adjustment Layer > Hue/Saturation. Click OK to accept the default name, Hue/Saturation 1. You'll notice that the selection marquee disappears in the image window, but don't worry, because it has already done its job.

6   Leave the Hue setting unchanged, but drag the Saturation slider to -20 and the Lightness setting to +5. Click OK.

Notice that the changes affect only the two selected blossoms, not the rest of the picture.

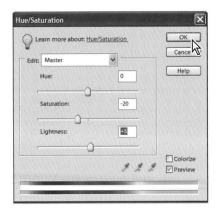

7   Choose File > Save. In the Save As dialog box, save the file in the My CIB Work folder, and name the file 05_03_Work.psd, accepting Photoshop (PSD) as the Format. If Save in Version Set with Original is selected, be sure to deselect it before you click Save.

If a message appears about maximizing compatibility, click OK to close it. Or, follow the instructions in the message to prevent it from appearing again.

As you can see, Photoshop Elements can dramatically improve images that you perceived as unsalvageable.

For complex selections, you can use keyboard shortcuts with selection tools instead of tool options bar icons to temporarily switch between New, Add, or Subtract selection modes. Hold down Shift to add, or Alt to subtract, as you click or drag the selection tool.

Comparing results of adjustment layers and auto fixes

You'll compare the manual adjustments you made with the results of the autofix you performed at the start of the lesson.

1　In Standard Edit mode, open the Autofix_05_03.jpg file in the My CIB Work folder by choosing File > Open and opening the file.

This is one of the files you fixed by applying the Auto Fix options at the beginning of the lesson. See "Getting started" at the beginning of this lesson, if you have not done that procedure.

Note: When the "Import Attached Tags" window appears, click on the check box next to Lesson 5 to include the lesson tag in your imported file.

2　Choose Window > Images > Tile to arrange the files in the work area.

3　Review the images to see the results achieved using different methods of correcting the files.

4　Choose File > Close All.

In this exercise, you've experienced the power and versatility of adjustment layers to alter lighting and color settings.

Correcting parts of an image

When you made color and lighting adjustments earlier in this lesson, they applied to the entire picture. Here you will adjust sections of an image.

Creating a selection

In this task, you'll select the area on the right side of the pillar where you see the leafy branches and sky. You'll begin by making a rectangular selection of most of the area and then adding details to that selection.

1   Switch to the Organizer, then click the 05_04.jpg image, the picture of the pillar, to select it. Choose Go to Standard Edit from the Edit menu in the shortcuts bar to open the image in Standard Edit mode.

2   In the toolbox, select the Rectangular Marquee tool (▭), which is grouped with the Elliptical Marquee tool (◯) in the toolbox.

3   Drag from the upper right corner to the bottom of the image, to the right of the pillar. Make sure that the selection rectangle fits snugly against the right side of the image.

4   Select the Magnetic Lasso tool (✒), which is grouped with the Lasso tool (◯) in the toolbox.

5 In the tool options bar, select Add to Selection (🖳).

Confirm the other (default) settings in the tool options bar, which should be Feather at 0 px, Width at 10 px, Edge Contrast at 10%, and Frequency at 57.

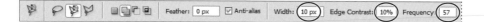

6 Click and release at the upper right corner of the selection rectangle to set an anchor point. Move the Magnetic Lasso across to the pillar and down its right edge.

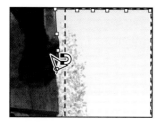

7 When you reach the bottom, click once. Move the cursor inside the lower left corner of the original selection rectangle. Double-click to complete the selection.

The Magnetic Lasso tool detects the edges of contrasting areas automatically but not perfectly. Keep the area selected and go on to the next procedure.

Refining and saving the selection

The Magnetic Lasso tool does an excellent job of selecting areas that contrast sharply with the surrounding area. For this image, the leaves in some areas have similar tonal values to the pillar, so you may need to do some clean-up work.

1   Select the Zoom tool (🔍) in the toolbox and then Zoom In (🔍) in the tool options bar. Zoom in so that you can see details of the selection you made in the previous procedure. If the selection is no longer active, repeat the previous procedure "Creating a selection."

2   Scroll up and down the right side of the image, looking for areas where the selection marquee does not line up with the edge of the pillar.

3   Select the Polygonal Lasso tool (🔾).

4   Remove any areas of the pillar that are included in the selection, as follows:

• Select Subtract from Selection (🔲) in the tool options bar.

• Click once to set a starting anchor point.

• Move the Polygonal Lasso tool a short distance along the edge of the pillar, and click again as needed to set additional anchor points.

• Double-click the tool to close the shape and complete the selection removal.

Note: *If moving the cursor continues to create a line in the image window, the selection is not closed. Try clicking the starting point of the selection, or double-clicking again to close it.*

Removing areas from the selection.

5 Add any areas of the trees that the selection missed, as follows:

• Select Add to Selection (◻) in the tool options bar.

• Click to set anchor points around the area that you want to add to the selection, and then close the selection.

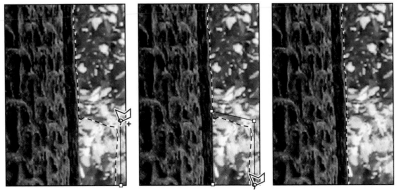

Adding to the selected area.

6 Choose Select > Save Selection.

7 In the Save Selection dialog box, type **Trees & Sky** to name the selection, and click OK. Saving the selection makes it easy to re-use it at a later time.

Correcting an overexposed area of the image

One of the aims in this exercise is to intensify the color and contrast in the overexposed area of the trees and sky. The pillar and shaded area are already a bit darker, so you won't want to adjust them. Your approach here is to divide and conquer—to apply different solutions to different areas of the image. Creating a copy of just the area you selected is the first step in this process.

1   In the Layers palette, click MORE in the upper right corner of the Layers palette to open the Layers palette menu, and choose Layers Palette Options.

2   Select the medium-sized thumbnail option, if it is not already selected, and click OK.

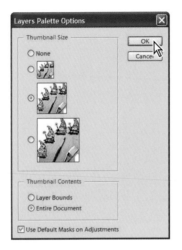

It's OK to select another size, but do not select None. The layer thumbnail can help you visualize the layers you will work with in this project.

3   Zoom out so that you can see the entire image, and then do one of the following:

• If the selection you made in the previous topic is still active, go to Step 4.

• If the selection is not active, choose Select > Load Selection. Make sure that Trees & Sky is selected, and click OK.

4   Choose Edit > Copy to copy the selected area.

5   Choose Edit > Paste to paste the copied area onto a new layer, Layer 1.

In the image window, the only difference you'll see is that the selection marquee has disappeared. But in the Layers palette, you can see that there's a new layer.

6 With Layer 1 (the copy of the tree and sky area) selected in the Layers palette, set the blending mode to Multiply. Now the trees and sky look more colorful.

Correcting an underexposed area with other blending modes

You can lighten the shadows of just the shaded areas with techniques that are similar to the ones you used to intensify the trees and sky.

1 In the Layers palette, select the Background layer.

2 Choose Select > Reselect, and then choose Select > Inverse.

Now the pillar and stucco wall are selected instead of the trees and sky.

Note: If you get a different selection or if the Reselect command is not available, choose Select > Load Selection, and then select the Invert option and Trees & Sky before completing Step 3.

3   Choose Edit > Copy and then choose Edit > Paste.

Note: If an error message appears saying that the selected area is empty, make sure that the Background layer is selected in the Layers palette, and try again.

4   With Layer 2 (the copy of the pillar and wall area) selected in the Layers palette, choose Screen as the blending mode. Notice that the pillar and wall are now brighter.

Adding more intensity and saving

Now the entire photograph looks much more lively. All that remains is to make any minor adjustments you like, and then see how this file compares to the one you automatically corrected at the beginning of this lesson.

1   Drag Layer 1 to the New Layer icon ([icon]) in the Layers palette to create a duplicate layer, Layer 1 Copy.

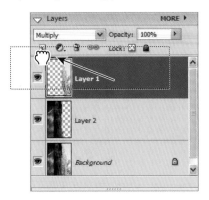

2 Drag Layer 2 to New Layer in the Layers palette to create a duplicate layer, Layer 2 Copy.

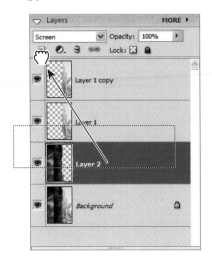

3 With Layer 2 Copy selected in the Layers palette, do the following:

• Choose Overlay as the blending mode.

• Click the arrow to the right of the Opacity setting to open the slider, and drag to 50%. Or type **50%**.

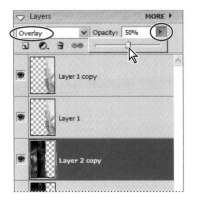

4 Examine the entire image, looking critically at the brightness and intensities in the different areas. Using your own judgment, adjust the opacity of the copied layers, Layer 1 copy and Layer 2 copy, to achieve the right balance in the image.

Note: You cannot change the Opacity or position of the Background layer, which is locked by default.

5   When you are satisfied with the results, choose File > Save.

6   In the Save As dialog box, save the file in the My CIB Work folder, naming the file 05_04_Work and accepting Photoshop (PSD) as the Format. If Save in Version Set with Original is selected, be sure to deselect it before you click Save.

If a message appears about maximizing compatibility, click OK to close it. Or, follow the instructions in the message to prevent it from appearing again

7   Leave the file open and go on to the next procedure.

Comparing your results to the auto-fixed version

Let's see how your careful work compares to the version you created earlier in this project.

1   In Standard Edit mode, use the File > Open command to locate and select the My CIB Work folder.

2   Double-click on the Autofix_05_04.jpg file to open it.

If the 05_04_Work.psd file is not still open from the previous procedure, double-click that file (in the same My CIB Work folder) to open it, too.

3   Arrange the files on top of each other, using Window > Images > Tile.

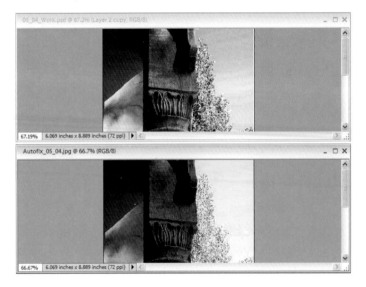

4   When you finish comparing the two results, choose File > Close All.

You've finished the final exercise in this lesson. In this exercise, you've learned how to use selections along with techniques you've practiced in other Lesson 5 exercises to correct images with complex exposure problems.

Saving and organizing your finished files

You're going to add tags to the work files, which were already added to the Organizer when you saved them, thanks to the Include in the Organizer option in the Save As dialog box.

1   Click Photo Browser ( ) on the Photoshop Elements Editor shortcuts bar to switch to the Organizer. If Back to All Photos appears on the Organizer shortcuts bar, select it.

2   Choose File > Get Photos > From Files and Folders. Go to the My CIB Work folder, and select the four auto-fixed files that you prepared at the beginning of Lesson 5. In the Import Attached Tags window, click Select All, then click OK. The files you created in this lesson are displayed.

Note: When the "Import Attached Tags" window appears, click the checkbox next to Lesson 5 to include the lesson tag in your imported file.

3   Choose Edit > Select All or press Ctrl+A to select all the thumbnails, and then drag the Work Files tag from the Tags palette to any one of the thumbnails to tag them all. Repeat this step to apply the Lesson 5 tag to your work files.

Note: If the Work Files tag doesn't appear in your Tags palette, see "Creating a tag for working files" in Lesson 2 for instructions on how to create it.

4   In the Organizer, click and then Ctrl+click to select all five versions of the Project 2 file, the sepia-toned image of the little boy.

5   Choose Edit > Stack > Stack Selected Photos to organize all the versions under one thumbnail.

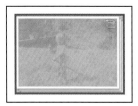

6   Repeat Steps 5 and 6 for the various versions of the other three projects.

You can now select Back to All Photos to see the entire catalog of thumbnails.

Congratulations! You've now finished Lesson 5. In this lesson, you've used a variety of methods for fixing images with exposure problems. You've used automatic fixes, layers with blending modes, adjustment layers, and a series of methods from the Enhance menu.

Review

► **Review questions**

1   Describe two ways to create an exact copy of an existing layer.

2   Where can you find the controls for adjusting the lighting in a photograph?

3   How do you change the arrangement of image windows in the work area?

4   What is an adjustment layer, and what are its unique benefits?

► **Review answers**

1   Photoshop Elements 4.0 must be running in Standard Edit mode to copy a layer. You can select the layer you want to duplicate in the Layers palette, and then choose Layer > Duplicate Layer. Alternatively, drag the layer to the New Layer button in the Layers palette. In either case, you get two identical layers, stacked one above the other.

2   You can adjust the lighting for a photo in either Standard Edit or Quick Fix mode. In Standard Edit, you must use the Enhance > Adjust Lighting menu to open various dialog boxes that contain the controls. Or, you can choose Enhance > Auto Levels, or Enhance > Auto Contrast. In Quick Fix mode, you can use the Lighting palette in the Palette Bin.

3   You cannot rearrange image windows in Quick Fix, which displays only one photograph at a time. In Standard Edit, there are several ways you can arrange them. One is to choose Window > Images, and choose one of the items listed there. Another method is to use the buttons in the upper right corner of the work area, just below the Minimize, Restore/Maximize, and Close buttons for Photoshop Elements 4.0. A third way is to drag the image window title bar to move an image window and to drag a corner to resize it (provided Maximize mode is not currently active).

4   An adjustment layer does not contain an image. Instead, it modifies some quality of all the layers below it in the Layer palette. For example, a Brightness/Contrast layer can alter the brightness and contrast of any underlying layers. One advantage of using an adjustment layer instead of adjusting an existing layer directly is that adjustment layers are easily reversible. You can click the eye icon for the adjustment layer to remove the effects instantly, and then restore the eye icon to apply the adjustments again. You can change a setting in the adjustment layer to zero to revert to its original condition.

6 | Repairing and Retouching Images

Images aren't always perfect. Maybe you want to delete the background, straighten an image, or merge several pictures to create a landscape. This lesson covers all this—and more.

In this lesson you will do the following:

- Straighten an image.

- Use the Magic Extractor command to remove a background.

- Merge photos into a panorama.

- Crop an image in both Standard Edit and Quick Fix modes.

- Remove wrinkles and skin flaws using the Healing brushes.

- Restore a damaged photograph.

- Use the Magic Selection brush to easily make a selection.

Most people can complete all the work in this lesson in 90 minutes or less. The lesson includes eight independent exercises, so you can do them all at once or in different work sessions. The projects vary in length and complexity. Some can be completed in less than five minutes, others can take 20 minutes or more.

Before you begin, make sure that you have accurately copied the project files from the CD attached to the inside back cover of this book. See "Copying the Classroom in a Book files" on page 3. Although you can do this lesson out of order, it requires some file structures, custom tags, and skills covered in Lessons 1 and 2.

In this lesson, you will use the CIB Catalog you created earlier in the book. If necessary, open this catalog by choosing File > Catalog in the Organizer, then click Open

Getting started

You can start with almost any of the exercises in this lesson, because most of them are independent of each other in both subject matter and skill level. Some preparation is necessary, however, before you begin to open the files for this lesson.

1 Start Photoshop Elements 4.0 in Standard Edit mode by choosing Edit and Enhance Photos from the Welcome Screen.

2 Open the Palette and Photo Bins, if they are not already open, by clicking the arrows ( ) and ( ) at the bottom of the work area or by choosing Window > Palette Bin and Window > Photo Bin to place check marks next to those commands.

3 Review the contents of the Palette Bin, making sure that the Layers, Navigator, Styles and Effects, and Undo History palettes are visible. If necessary, open any of these palettes from the Window menu.

Note: For help with Palette Bin contents, see "Using the Palette Bin" in Lesson 3, "Sharing Creations."

4 Click on the Photo Browser button ( ) to go to the Organizer. If the CIB Catalog is not already open, choose File > Catalog > Open, select CIB Catalog, and click Open.

Straightening an image

Unless you use a tripod, it's nearly impossible to keep a camera completely still when taking a picture. The result of this movement is often an image that is not perfectly straight. Photoshop Elements allows you to correct crooked images with ease.

Using the Straighten tool

The Straighten tool allows you to manually specify a new straight edge, which Photoshop Elements then uses as a reference to straighten the image.

1 In the Tags palette, click the Find box for the Lesson 6 tags.

2 Locate and select the 06_01.jpg file, which is a picture of an estate house.

3 Click Edit > Go to Standard Edit.

4 Select the Straighten tool ( ).

5   Choose Crop to Remove Background from the Canvas Options drop-down menu
in the tool options bar.

This will remove any extra canvas area from the image as it's rotated, matching the
straight edge you specified.

Note: In a multi-layered file, you can use the Rotate All Layers option.

6   With the Straighten tool, draw a line from left to right in the image that is parallel
with the roof line of the building. This represents your new straight edge.

7   When you release the mouse, Photoshop Elements straightens the image relative to
the edge you've just drawn.

8   Choose File > Save As, and save the straightened file as **06_01_Work** in the My
CIB Work folder you created. If Save in Version Set with Original is selected, be sure to
deselect it before you click Save. Click OK in the JPEG options window to accept the
default settings.

9   Close the file.

💡 *For some images, you may want to consider using the Image > Rotate > Straighten
Image or Image > Rotate > Straighten and Crop Image commands, which perform
straightening functions automatically.*

In the next exercise, you'll remove a background from an image by extracting its foreground.

Using the Magic Extractor to remove a background

You can use the Magic Extractor command to make quick and accurate selections based on areas that you specify. You can specify these areas simply by placing colored dots, or by dragging the mouse in the areas you want to mark for removal. After you mark the areas, only the foreground appears in the photo.

The Magic Extractor makes it easy to select people or objects in your photos so that you can superimpose them onto other backgrounds. You can then save the extracted image as a new file. Your original photo remains intact and untouched.

1   If necessary, click Photo Browser to return to the Organizer. Only the images with Lesson 6 tags should be visible.

2   Locate the image of the boy with the red hat eating ice cream. Select the image. In the shortcuts bar, click Edit and choose Go to Standard Edit.

3   Choose Image > Magic Extractor. The Magic Extractor window opens.

4   Select the Foreground Brush tool (✎) and click with your mouse to paint over the figure of the boy in the foreground of this image. This defines, in red, the area that you want to select and extract. It is not necessary to cover everything that is to be extracted. Clicking and dragging over some portion of the shirt, hat, face, arm and ice cream cone is sufficient.

Specify a different brush size or color for either brush by doing any of the following:

•   To change the brush size, choose a new size from the Brush Size menu.

•   To change the color of either the Foreground or Background Brush tool, click the Foreground Color swatch or the Background Color swatch and choose a new color in the color picker; then click OK.

💡 *Use the Zoom tool to increase the magnification of the image. Press the spacebar to scroll while viewing at an increased magnification. Press the Alt key when using the Zoom tool to reduce your magnification.*

5   Select the Background Brush tool (✐) and click with your mouse to identify the background of this image. This defines the area in blue that you do not want included in your selection. A few quick clicks over the sky, grass, tree and pagoda are all that you need to identify the background.

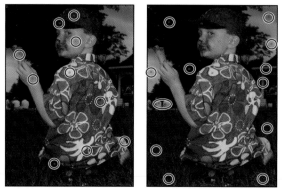

Foreground selections.   *Background selections.*

Note: *When selecting objects with varied colors and textures, additional dots make a more accurate selection.*

6   Click Preview to see the current selection. You may need to wait while the preview is generated.

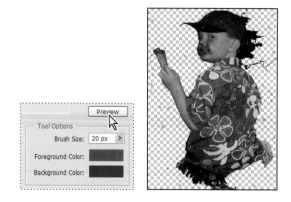

You can change the preview settings by doing either of the following in the Magic Extractor window:

•   To change what is displayed in the Preview area, choose either Selection Area or Original Photo from the Display menu.

•   To specify a different background for the selection, choose an option from the Background menu.

7   If the boy in the foreground is not completely extracted from the image, you can edit your selection. Do any of the following to fine-tune the selection:

• To add areas to a selection, use the Add to Selection tool (⟨🖋⟩) and click or drag over the area you want to add to your selection.

• To remove areas from the current selection, select the Remove from Selection tool (⟨🖉⟩) and drag over the areas in your current selection that you do not want to be part of your selection.

• To smooth the edges of your foreground selection, select the Smoothing Brush tool (⟨✐⟩) and drag over the areas you want to smooth.

• To remove fringe colors left between the foreground and background, click the Defringe button. To increase or decrease the amount of fringe removed, specify a value from the Defringe Width menu.

• If you make a mistake or want to start over, click Reset to remove all marks.

8   Click OK to accept the selection and close the Magic Extractor window. The selected image appears as a new file in the Editor window.

9   Press Ctrl+A on your keyboard to select the extracted image, then choose Ctrl+C to copy the image. You will be pasting the image into a different photo.

10   Press the Photo Browser button to return to the Organizer and choose 06_01_ Work.jpg—the picture of the estate that you straightened earlier in this lesson. Choose Go to Standard Edit from the Edit menu in the shortcuts bar.

11   Choose Edit > Paste to paste the picture of the boy eating ice cream in front of the estate.

12 Choose the Move tool. Press and hold the shift key while clicking and dragging the handle on the upper left corner point. Drag down and to the right to reduce the size of the image.

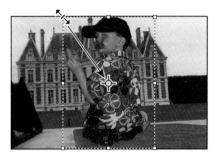

13 If desired, reposition the boy on the lawn, then click the Commit button (✔).

14 Choose File > Save.

Save this file as **06_02_Work**. Select the My CIB Work folder as the location. If Save in Version Set with Original is selected, be sure to deselect it. Leave other default settings and click Save.

15 Close the file of the boy without saving changes.

Note: The Magic Extractor tool works especially well on pictures with a clearly defined background, and often requires little or no cleanup work. You can practice using the tool with some of the pictures of the airplanes in flight that you used in Lesson 3, and copying the images into other pictures.

Merging photos into a panorama

The four photos you'll use for the next exercise are incremental views of a river running through farmland. This is an ideal opportunity for learning how to create panoramas because of the strong, distinctive lines made by roads running between the fields. You'll use those roads as a guide for perfecting the orientation and placement of the photos, but only after Photoshop Elements does most of the work for you.

1 If you are not already in Standard Edit after completing the previous exercise, choose Edit > Go to Standard Edit.

2 In Standard Edit, choose File > New > Photomerge™ Panorama.

3 Click Browse in the dialog box that opens and go to the Lesson06 folder.

4   For this exercise, the photomerge works best if the files are in alphabetical order. Select 06_03A and click Open. Browse and add 06_03B, 06_03C, and 06_03D, in that order, one at a time. After the four files are listed in the Photomerge window, in the correct order, click OK.

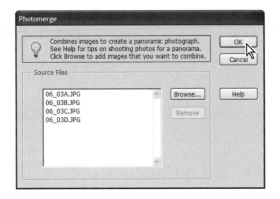

Note: *You can also start the photomerge process in the Organizer. Find and select the thumbnails of the individual photographs that make up the panorama, and select them. Then choose File > New > Photomerge™ Panorama. Photoshop Elements automatically switches to Standard Edit and opens the Photomerge dialog box. Click OK to confirm your selected files.*

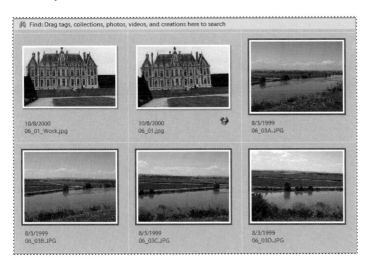

Wait while Photoshop Elements opens and closes windows to create the panorama. If a message appears telling you that some images could not be automatically arranged, follow the instructions for arranging them manually.

5   In the large Photomerge window, do the following to fine-tune the panorama, if necessary:

•   Using the Select Image tool (↖), select the second photo from the left.

•   Select the Rotate Image tool (⟳), and drag counter-clockwise to rotate the second photo, so that the road in the distance is parallel with its position in the picture to the right.

Note: It may help to click the Snap to Image check box to deselect it and to zoom in, using the Zoom tool (🔍) in the upper left side of the dialog box.

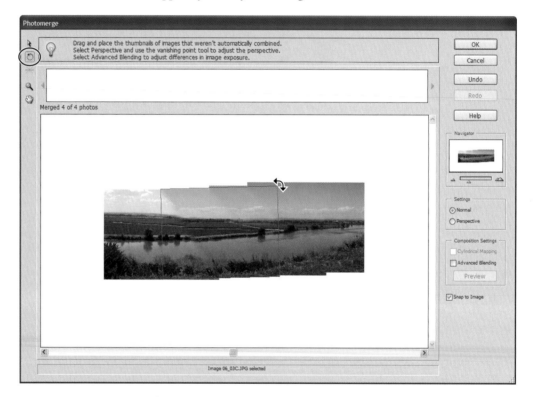

•   Switch back to the Select Image tool and drag the second picture down slightly so that the roads in the two center pictures line up perfectly. (As you drag the image, its appearance becomes semi-transparent so that you see the underlying area of the third photograph.)

•   Repeat the process of rotating the image for the picture on the far left so that the road aligns with the road in the second picture.

6   When you are satisfied with the results, click the Advanced Blending checkbox, and then click Preview.

7   After examining the preview, click Exit Preview. Then click OK.

The Photomerge dialog box closes, and Photoshop Elements goes to work. You'll see windows open and close as you wait for Photoshop Elements to create the panorama.

Cropping images

The Crop tool removes part of an image outside a selected area. Cropping is useful when you want to focus on a certain area of your photo. When you crop a photo, the resolution remains the same as in the original photo.

Since the photos that you just merged do not match precisely, you'll use the Crop tool to create a uniform edge.

1 Select the Crop tool (⌗) and drag a cropping selection around the image, being careful not to include any of the checkerboard areas where the image is transparent. Then click the Commit button in the lower right corner of the image.

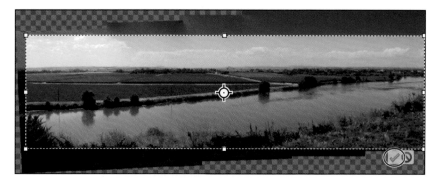

Note: The Crop tool can also be used in Quick Fix mode.

Though it's not required for this image, you can specify any of the following settings in the options bar when cropping:

- The Aspect Ratio setting allows you to specify a preset crop. No Restriction lets you resize the image to any dimension. Use Photo Ratio retains the aspect ratio of the photo when you crop.

- The sizes listed specify preset sizes for the cropped photo. If you want your final output to be a specific size, such as 4 x 6 to fit a picture frame, choose that preset size.

- The Width and Height fields allow you to specify the physical dimensions of the image.

2 Choose File > Save, and save the merged image in the My CIB Work folder as **06_03_Work**, and select JPEG as the Format. If Save in Version Set with Original is selected, be sure to deselect it before you click Save. After you click Save, the JPEG Options dialog box appears. For Quality, select 12, Maximum, and click OK. Close the file, and any other files that are open.

Vanishing Point

A vanishing point is the point at which receding parallel lines seem to meet when seen in perspective. For example, as a road stretches out in front of you, it will seem to grow thinner the farther away it is, until it is almost nonexistent on the horizon. This is the vanishing point.

You can add this perspective to images using Photoshop Elements. Repeat the panorama procedure up to Step 4. Then, instead of moving and rotating the images to get the roads aligned, select Perspective in the Photomerge dialog box. Select the Vanishing Point tool ( ) and click near the far right side of the image, just above the horizon. Don't forget to select Advanced Blending before you click OK.

Panorama perspective with reset vanishing point, and cropped version of the same image.

Removing wrinkles and spots

Retouching photographs is both a skilled craft and an art. In this exercise, you'll try several ways to smooth out laugh lines and wrinkles, and blend skin tones.

Preparing the file for editing

Before you actually start retouching, you'll set up the layers you need to do the work. By saving the file with a new name, you'll make it easy to identify it later as your work file.

1   Using the Organizer, find and open the 06_04.jpg file, which is tagged for Lesson 6. It is a picture of a woman with her grandchild. Choose Edit > Go to Standard Edit.

2   In the Layers palette, drag the Background layer to the New Layer button (⬚) in the Layers palette to create another new layer, Background Copy.

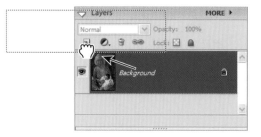

3   Choose File > Save As, and then save the file in Photoshop (PSD) format as **06_04_Work**. Select the My CIB Work folder as the location. If Save in Version Set with Original is selected, be sure to deselect it before you click Save.

Now you're ready to start working.

Using the Healing Brush tool

You're going to create smoother skin and natural-looking skin tones using the Healing Brush tool.

1   You'll want to zoom in on the upper half of the photo, as you'll be retouching the woman's face, neck, and shoulder.

2   Select the Healing Brush tool, which is grouped with the Spot Healing Brush tool in the toolbox.

3   In the tool options bar, select the following options:

• For Brush, click the small arrow to open the palette and set the Diameter at 15 px.

• For Mode, select Normal.

• For Source, select Sampled.

• Deselect Aligned and Sample All Layers if they are selected.

4   Alt+click the Healing Brush tool on the woman's left cheek to establish that area as the reference texture.

Note: Until you perform this essential step, the Healing Brush tool can't work. If you switch to another tool and then back to the Healing Brush, you must repeat this step.

5   Drag a short distance under the eyes. As you drag, it looks as if you're painting dark spots, but when you release the mouse button, the highlight color disappears and skin tones fill in the area.

Note: Be very careful to keep your brush strokes short. Longer strokes may produce unacceptable results. If that happens, choose Edit > Undo Healing Brush or use the Undo History palette to backtrack. Or, try just clicking instead of dragging. Also, make sure that Aligned is not selected in the tool options bar.

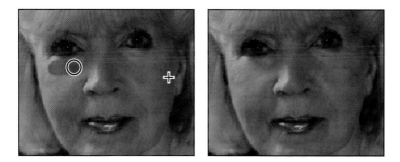

6   Continue to use the Healing Brush to smooth the skin on the face, and hands. Avoid the areas close to the eyes or near the edges of the face. Feel free to re-establish the area by Alt+clicking in other parts of the face to use different skin tones.

Use the Undo History palette to quickly undo a series of steps. Every action you perform on the file is recorded in chronological order from top to bottom of the palette. To restore the file to an earlier state, simply select that action in the Undo History palette. If you change your mind before making any other changes, you can select a later step in the Undo History palette and restore the image to that phase of your work.

The Healing Brush tool copies texture, not color. In this case, it samples the colors from the area it brushes and arranges those colors according to the texture of the reference area (the cheek). Consequently, the Healing Brush tool appears to be smoothing the skin. So far, the results are not convincingly realistic, but you'll work on that in the next topic.

Using the Spot Healing Brush

An alternative to the Healing Brush, the Spot Healing Brush removes imperfections in your photos more quickly than you can with the Healing Brush. You can either click, or click and drag to smooth away imperfections in an area.

In this part of the exercise, you'll use the Spot Healing Brush to blend the skin tones on the neck and shoulder.

1 In the Editor, select the Spot Healing Brush tool, which is grouped with the Healing Brush tool.

2 Choose a brush size. A brush that is slightly larger than the area you want to fix works best, so that you can cover the entire area with one click. A setting of 15 px works well for this example.

3 Choose Proximity Match in the tool options bar. This option uses the pixels around the edge of the selection to find an image area to use as a patch for the selected area. If this option doesn't provide a satisfactory fix, undo the fix and try the Create Texture option, which uses all the pixels in the selection to create a texture in which to fix the area.

4   Click on the darker skin tones on the neck to blend these areas. Click and drag to blend them into the lighter parts of the skin.

Note: If the Spot Healing Brush doesn't work, try dragging through the area a second time.

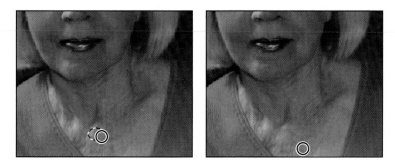

Refining the healing work

In this topic, you'll use another texture tool to finish your work on this image.

1   Use the Navigator palette to zoom in and shift the focus to the eye area of the woman's face.

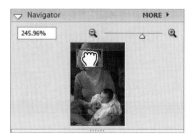

2   Select the Blur tool. Then set the brush diameter in the tool options bar to approximately 13 px.

3   Drag the Blur tool over the laugh lines around the eyes and mouth.

4   In the tool options bar, reduce the Blur tool brush diameter to 7 px. Drag across the lips to smooth them out, avoiding the edges.

5   Using the Healing Brush and Blur tools, continue working on the image until you have eliminated most of the lines, and blended the skin tones. Use the Navigator palette to change the zoom level and shift the focus as needed.

6   In the Layers palette, change the Opacity of the Background Copy layer to about 70%, using your own judgment to set the exact percentage.

Compare your results to the original, retouched (100% Opacity), and final results illustrated below.

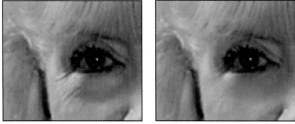

Before.   *After.*

7   Choose File > Save to replace your work file, and then close the file.

Extensive retouching can leave skin looking artificially smooth, like molded plastic. Reducing the opacity of the retouched layer gives the skin a more realistic look by allowing some of the texture on the original Background layer to show through. Although they are slightly visible, they are softened.

In this exercise, you learned how to set an appropriate source for the Healing Brush tool, and then use the texture of that source to repair flaws in another area of the photograph. You also used the Spot Healing Brush to quickly smooth and blend the skin in the neck and shoulder. Lastly, you used the Blur tool to smooth textures, and finished with an opacity change, to create a more realistic look.

Note: You can enable or disable the retouched Background copy layer to compare the original file with your edited version.

Restoring a damaged photograph

All sorts of nasty things can happen to precious old photographs—or precious new photographs, for that matter. The scanned image you'll use in this project is challenging, because of a large crease in the original print, and other flaws.

With Photoshop Element 4.0 tools and features, you have the power to restore this picture to a convincing simulation of its original condition. There's no magic pill that fixes significant damage in one or two keystrokes. For important heirloom pictures, it's worth the effort, and we think you'll be impressed with what you can accomplish in this project.

Preparing a working copy of the image file

Your first job is to set up the file and layers for the work you'll do in this project.

1 Using the Organizer, find the 06_05 file which is an old picture of a boy and girl. Choose Edit > Go to Standard Edit.

2 Choose File > Save As.

3 In the Save As dialog box, type **06_05_Work** as the File Name and select Photoshop (PSD) as the Format. For Save In, select the My CIB Work folder. If Save in Version Set with Original is selected, be sure to deselect it before you click Save.

4 Choose Layer > Duplicate Layer and click OK to accept the default name.

5 Choose File > Save.

Using the Selection Brush tool

The first thing you'll do with this project is to use the Dust & Scratches filter to remove the stray dots and frayed edges of the scanned image. This filter smooths out the pixels in a way that puts the image just slightly out of focus. That's OK for the background, but you want to keep the subject matter—the children—as detailed and sharp as possible.

To do that, you'll need to create a selection that includes only the areas you want to blur.

1 In the toolbox, select the Selection Brush tool (✎)—it may be beneath the Magic Selection Brush tool (✎). Be careful not to select a painting brush tool by mistake.

2 In the tool options bar, select a round brush shape and about 60 pixels for Size. You may need to increase the brush size after the previous exercise.

Leave the other options at the default values: Mode should be set to Selection and Hardness should be set to 100%.

3   Drag the brush along the frayed edges of the photograph to select those areas. Then increase the brush size to approximately 100 pixels, and continue painting the selection to include all the frayed edges and most of the backdrop behind the children.

Note: Don't try to be too precise; it's OK if some of your strokes slop over onto the children because you'll fix that in the next topic.

4   Choose Select > Save Selection.

5   Name the new selection **Backdrop**, and click OK to close the dialog box.

The Selection Brush tool is an intuitive way to create a complex selection. It is especially useful in images like this one, where there are no unique color blocks, few sharp boundaries between pictured items, and few crisp geometric shapes.

What is a mask?

A mask is the opposite of a selection. The selection is the area that you can alter; everything outside the selection is unaffected by editing changes. A mask is the area that's protected from changes, just like the solid areas of a stencil or the masking tape you'd put on window glass before you paint the trim on your home.

Another difference between a mask and a selection is the way Photoshop Elements presents them visually. You're familiar with the flashing line of black and white dashes that signal a selection marquee. A mask appears as a colored, semi-transparent overlay on the image. You can change the color of the mask overlay using the Overlay Color option that appears in the tool options bar when the Selection Brush tool is set to operate in Mask mode.

Another advantage of the Selection Brush tool is that it is very forgiving. For example, you can hold down Alt to remove areas from a selection. Or, you can use the tool in Mask mode, which is another intuitive way of adding to the areas outside the selection, as you'll try next.

Using the Magic Selection Brush

Just as the Spot Healing Brush provides a quicker alternative to the Healing Brush tool, the Magic Selection Brush (✐) is a faster alternative to using the Selection Brush. You simply draw, scribble, or click the area you want to select; the definition of the selection doesn't need to be precise. When you release the mouse, Photoshop Elements draws the selection border.

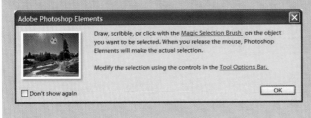

Refining a saved selection

As you progress through this book, you are gathering lots of experience with saving selections. In this procedure, you'll amend a saved selection. You'll replace the original, saved selection with your improved version.

1   In the work area, make sure that:

• The Backdrop selection is still active in the image window. If it is not active, choose Selection > Load Selection, and choose the saved selection by name before clicking OK.

• The Selection Brush tool (✐) is still selected in the toolbox.

2 In the tool options bar, select Mask in the Mode drop-down menu.

You now see a semi-transparent, colored overlay in the unselected areas of the image. This represents the image mask, which covers the protected areas.

3 Examine the image, looking for unmasked areas with details that should be protected, such as places where the Selection Brush strokes lapped over onto the children.

Use the Navigator palette slider or Zoom tool (⊕) to adjust your view of the image, if necessary.

4 Reduce the brush size of the Selection Brush to about 30 px, then use the brush to paint to include any areas you want to mask. Press the Alt key while painting to remove the mask.

In this mode, the Selection Brush tool adds to the mask rather than to the selection.

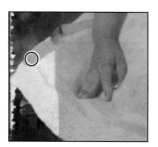

5 Switch back and forth between Selection and Mask modes, making corrections until you are satisfied with the selection.

Your goal is to mask areas that contain fine details, even those caught in the crease. Although these are damaged, you can take advantage of the details that have survived.

6 Choose Select > Save Selection.

In the Save Selection dialog box, choose Backdrop from the Selection drop-down menu. Then, under Operation, select Replace Selection, and click OK. Keep the selection active for the next procedure.

Filtering flaws out of the backdrop area

Now that you've made your selection, you're ready to apply the filter that will soften the selected areas, reducing the tiny scratches and dust specs.

1 If the Backdrop selection is no longer active, choose Select > Load Selection, and choose Backdrop before you click OK to close the dialog box.

2 Choose Filter > Noise > Dust & Scratches.

3 In the dialog box, make sure that Preview is selected, and then drag the Radius slider to 7 pixels and the Threshold slider to 10 levels. Move the dialog box so that you can see most of the image window, but do not close it yet.

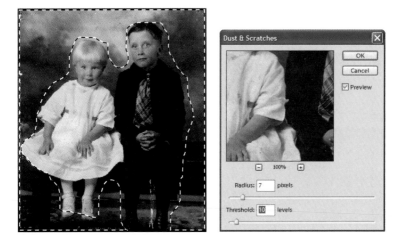

4 Examine the results in the image window. The frayed edges of the image should be repaired and the stray dust and tiny scratches eliminated. Move the cursor inside the thumbnail and drag with the hand icon to change the preview area that is displayed.

5 Make adjustments to the Radius and Threshold values until you are satisfied with the results, then click OK.

6 Choose Select > Deselect, and choose File > Save to save your work.

The Dust & Scratches filter does a good job of clearing away spots created by flaws on the negative. However, it doesn't repair damage to the areas outside the selection.

Using the Clone Stamp tool to fill in missing areas

The Clone Stamp tool works in ways similar to the Healing Brush tool that you used in the previous exercise. The Clone Stamp tool copies the source area—not just texture—and places it in the areas where you drag.

In this procedure, you'll use the Clone Stamp tool to fill in missing details in the image from other parts of the picture.

1   Using the Navigator palette or the Zoom tool, zoom in and focus on the area showing the boy's legs and feet, which is damaged by a heavy crease.

2   In the toolbox, select the Clone Stamp tool, which is grouped with the Pattern Stamp tool. On the left end of the tool options bar, click the tool icon, and choose Reset Tool from the drop-down menu.

Reset Tool reinstates the default values—Size: 21 px, Mode: Normal, Opacity: 100%, and the Aligned option is selected.

3   Move the Clone Stamp tool so that it is centered at the edge of the shaded area between the boy's shoes. Hold down the Alt key and click to set the source position. Centering the source on a horizontal line makes it easier to line up the brush for cloning.

Note: If necessary, you can reset the source by Alt+clicking again in a different location.

4   Move the brush over the damaged area so that it is centered at the same horizontal position as the source reference point. Click and drag upwards a short distance to copy the source image onto the damaged area.

As you drag, crosshairs appear, indicating where the source is—that is, the area that the Clone Stamp tool is copying.

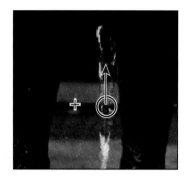

5   Click and drag the brush vertically over the crease-damaged area until the repair is complete.

The crosshairs follow the movement of the brush. Because you selected the Aligned option in the tool options bar, the crosshairs maintain the same distance and angle to the brush that you set when you made the first brush stroke.

6   Choose File > Save to replace your work file, or click the Save button (![save]).

Cleaning the girl's shoes

Through no fault of the photographer, the white shoes on the little girl appear scuffed and dirty. You'll tidy them up with the Dodge tool.

The Dodge tool and its opposite, the Burn tool, derive their names from traditional darkroom techniques for controlling the exposure for different areas of an image. In this task, you'll use the electronic equivalent of dodging—reducing the exposure for a limited area of the light-sensitive photographic paper.

1   Using the Navigator palette or scroll bars, shift the focus to the little girl's feet. Keep the magnification so that you can easily see details, such as the texture of her stockings.

2   In the toolbox, select the Dodge tool.

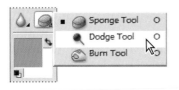

3   In the tool options bar, select a soft round brush and set the Size to a small diameter, such as 19 pixels. Make sure that Midtones and 50% Exposure are selected.

4   Click and drag the Dodge tool across one of the dirty toes on the girl's shoes, using short brush strokes.

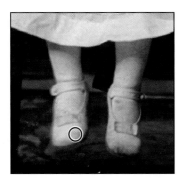

5   Continue to apply the Dodge tool until the toes of the shoes look about the same as the clean parts.

Finishing up the project

While you could spend longer working on this picture, the quality now is acceptable for most purposes. You'll fix just a few more areas before leaving this project.

1   Double-click the Hand tool (✋) to zoom out so that you can see the entire image. Alternatively, you can use the Navigator palette or the Zoom tool.

2   Examine the entire image, looking for dark or light flecks created by dust on the negative, especially on the boy's jacket.

3   In the toolbox, select the Blur tool (◌), and type **40 px** for Size in the tool options bar.

4   Click or drag the tool over any dust spots to blend them into the area surrounding them.

5   Review all areas of the image. If you see flaws that you want to fix, use the Blur tool, Dodge tool, or Clone Stamp tool to make any additional repairs or corrections you desire.

6   Choose File > Save, and then close the file.

Congratulations, you have finished this project. In this exercise, you've used blurring and a filter to hide spots, flecks, and texture flaws. You've also cloned one area of an image to repair an area that's been damaged. You've used the Selection Brush tool to create selections in two modes: Selection and Mask. Along the way, you've seen how to reset a tool to its default settings.

Review

▶ Review questions

1   Describe three ways to straighten a crooked image.

2   In the Photomerge dialog box, which tools can be used to fine-tune a panorama created from multiple images, and how do they work?

3   What are the similarities and differences between using the Healing Brush and the Spot Healing Brush tools to retouch photos?

4   Why is it necessary to make a selection (e.g., using the Magic Selection tool) before applying the Dust & Scratches filter to restore a damaged photograph?

▶ Review answers

1   One method to straighten an image is to use the Image > Rotate > Straighten Image command to automatically straighten the image. A similar method is to use the Image > Rotate > Straighten and Crop Image command, which crops the image as it straightens. A third method is to select the Straighten tool and draw a new straight edge in the image. When you finish drawing and release the mouse, Photoshop Elements straightens the image relative to the new edge.

2   The Select Image tool is used to select a specific image from within the merged panorama. It can also be used to drag an image so that it lines up more exactly with the other images in the panorama. The Rotate Image tool is used to rotate merged images so that their content aligns seamlessly.

3   Both tools copy from one part of an image to another. The Spot Healing Brush tool, especially with the Proximity Match option selected, allows you to remove blemishes more quickly than does the Healing Brush, because it only involves clicking and/or dragging on an imperfection to smooth it. The Healing Brush is more customizable, but requires Alt+clicking to establish a reference texture.

4   Because the Dust & Scratches filter smooths out pixels in an image by putting them slightly out of focus, you'll want to create a selection that includes only the areas you want to blur. Otherwise, your subject matter won't be as detailed and sharp as possible.

7 | Working with Text

You can expand your creative work by incorporating text into your images using Photoshop Elements 4.0. In this lesson, you'll learn how to do the following:

- Add a border to an image by changing the canvas size.

- Use Creations to enhance the appearance of your photos.

- Select a tool and change its settings in the tool options bar.

- Format, add, and edit text.

- Manipulate text using special effects.

- Apply Layer Styles to text.

- Move image layers independently.

- Hide and reveal layers.

- Transfer a layer from one image to another.

- Add a Shape layer.

- Merge two layers into a single layer.

- Use the Creations features to build a project.

- Create a simple animation.

- Optimize images for maximum efficiency and Web distribution.

Before you begin, make sure that you've correctly copied the project files from the *Adobe Photoshop Elements 4.0 Classroom in a Book* CD (attached to the inside of the back cover of this book). See "Copying the Classroom in a Book files" on page 3.

In this lesson, you will use the CIB Catalog you created earlier in the book. If necessary, open this catalog by choosing File > Catalog in the Organizer, then click Open.

Getting started

This lesson includes five projects. Each project builds on the skills learned in the ones before it. Most people need about half an hour to complete each of the five projects, so you might plan to complete the lesson in more than one work session.

This lesson assumes that you are already familiar with general features of the Photoshop Elements 4.0 work area and that you recognize the two ways in which you can use Photoshop Elements: the Editor and the Organizer. If you discover that you need more background information as you proceed, see Photoshop Elements Help or the Tutorials available on the Welcome Screen.

Placing a text label on an image

This project will involve typing, formatting, and arranging text on an existing photograph. The goal is to add text to mark the occasion of a wedding and create a decorative border for the photo so it can be printed and mounted in a picture frame.

The original file (left) and completed project file (right).

Using the Organizer to find and open tagged files

To make it easier to find the files you'll work with, we've tagged them with the appropriate project name.

1   Open the Organizer.

2   Make sure that the Organize Bin is open, so that you can see the list of Tags. Or, open it now by clicking the Organize Bin arrow in the lower right corner of the work area.

3 Click the Lesson 7 tag Find box, located to the left of the name Lesson 7 in the Tags palette under the Imported Tags. Now the thumbnails show only the image files that you'll use in this lesson.

4 Click the Project 1 Find box. Only one image is tagged with both the Lesson 7 and Project 1 tags, so only one thumbnail appears.

5 Select the thumbnail and then click Edit in the shortcuts bar, and choose Go to Standard Edit.

Adding an uneven border

In this procedure, you'll enlarge the canvas—the area on which the image appears—without increasing the size of the image. The canvas size is usually the same as the image size for digital photographs, but you can enlarge it to add a border. The border area takes on the Background color, which is comparable to the paper underlying a photographic print.

In this procedure, you'll create this border in two phases and give it precise dimensions.

1   In the Photoshop Elements 4.0 Editor with the bride.jpg file open, choose Image > Resize > Canvas Size.

2   In the Canvas Size dialog box, complete the following steps:

• Select the Relative check box.

• For Width, type **1** and select inches from the drop-down menu.

• For Height, type **1** and select inches from the drop-down menu.

• Click to select the center square in the Anchor diagram.

• Choose White for the Canvas extension color.

• Click OK to close the dialog box and apply the changes. A uniformly sized white border now surrounds the image.

3   Choose Image > Resize > Canvas Size again. Confirm that the Relative checkbox remains selected, and then enter the following options:

- In the Anchor diagram, select the center square in the top row.

- Confirm Width is set to 0, or enter **0** now.

- For Height, type **0.75**.

- Leave all other settings unchanged, and click OK.

Now the border has grown taller but only in the area under the image.

Adding a decorative border

Before we add the text to mark the occasion, we'll have to establish a border so we know how large of an area we'll have for adding type. This can be accomplished using some of the built-in frame effects.

1   Locate the Styles and Effects palette along the right side of the Photoshop Elements Editor window. If necessary, you can open the palette by choosing Window > Styles and Effects.

2   In the Styles and Effects window, choose Effects in the drop-down menu on the left side of the window and frames in the drop-down menu on the right side of the window.

3   Browse the frames from the list and click once to choose the Brushed Aluminum Frame.

4 Drag the frame from the Styles and Effects window, and drop it on the picture of the bride. You can also double-click the frame.

Note: This creates two new layers, one is a copy of the original background layer, and the other is a new layer that includes the frame.

Adding a quick border

When precision isn't important for the canvas-size enlargement, you can use the Crop tool to quickly add a border to an image.

1 Select the Zoom tool ( ) and zoom out by holding down the Alt key and clicking. The cursor will change from a magnifying glass with a plus sign ( ) to one with a minus sign ( ). If necessary, click again until you can see some of the gray pasteboard surrounding the image.

2 Select the Crop tool ( ) and drag a rectangle within the image—size doesn't matter at this point.

3 Drag the corner handles of the crop marquee outside the image area onto the pasteboard to define the size and shape of border that you want to create.

4 After you have defined the new size for the image and border, click the Commit button ( ) on the tool options bar to apply the change. Or, click the Cancel button ( ) next to the Commit button if you don't want to crop the image. The Background Color fills in the newly expanded canvas.

Formatting and typing a text layer

Now you will use the tool options bar to set up text formatting. This includes the font family, font size, text color, and other text attributes. The tool options bar changes based upon the active tool.

1   In the toolbox, select the Horizontal Type tool (T).

2   In the tool options bar, select the following from the drop-down menus:

-   For font family, select a cursive, script font, such as Brush Script.

-   For font size, select 48 pt.

3   Click in the frame area below the picture to set the cursor, and type **Gwyn's Wedding Day**.

Note: Don't worry about the exact position of the text in the image or any typing errors, because you'll correct those later in this project.

4   Click the Commit button (✔) in the tool options bar to accept the text. Or, press Enter on the numeric keypad.

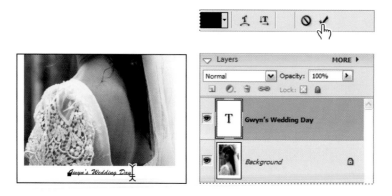

Note: Do not press the Enter or Return keys on the central part of your keyboard to accept text changes. When the Type tool is active, these keys add a line break in the text.

5   Select the Move tool (▸⊕) in the toolbox.

6   Place the cursor inside the text so that the cursor turns into a solid black arrowhead (▸) and drag the text so that it is visually centered along the lower border of the image.

7   Locate the Layers palette in the Palette Bin on the right side of the work area. Scroll through the layers and notice that the image is now made up of four layers: a Background, Layer 2 (which is a copy of the Background), a text layer, and Layer 1, which contains the frame. Most of the text layer is transparent, so only the text itself blocks your view of the Background layer.

Diagram of the layer structure, and Layers palette.

Note: *Adobe Photoshop Elements 4.0 also includes other tools for adding text to your images. Throughout the remainder of this lesson, the term Type tool always refers to the Horizontal Type tool, which is the default type tool.*

Editing a text layer

Adding text is a nondestructive process, so your original image is not overwritten by the text. If you save your file in the native Photoshop (PSD) format, you can reopen it and move, edit, or delete the text layer without hurting the image.

Using the Type tool is much like typing in a word-processing application. If you want to change attributes, such as font or color, select the characters you want to change, and then adjust the settings.

1   If necessary, choose View > Zoom In to enlarge the image until you can comfortably read the text you added in the previous exercise.

2   Confirm that the text layer Gwyn's Wedding Day is selected in the Layers palette and that the Type tool (T) is selected.

3   Click to the right of the word "Day" and add a space, then – **July 28th, 2005** so that the text line reads: "Gwyn's Wedding Day – July 28th, 2005".

4   Move the cursor to the beginning of the text. Click and drag over the text to select all the text.

5   In the tool options bar, click the arrow beside the Color option and select a dark red color swatch. When choosing your own colors, be certain to select colors that are easy to read against the background color. Press the Return key to close the Swatches palette.

Note: If you accidentally click the Color sample instead of the arrow in the tool options bar, you'll open the Color Picker, which is a different way to select colors.

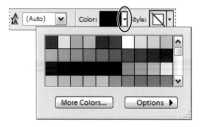

6   Select the Move tool. Click and drag to center the text, zooming out if necessary, to see more of the image.

7 If necessary, using the Type tool, correct any typing errors you may have made by:

• Clicking once to move the insertion point to another position within the text, or using the arrow keys to move the cursor forward or back.

• Clicking and dragging to select multiple characters.

• Typing to add text or to overwrite selected characters.

• Pressing Backspace or Delete to erase characters.

8 Click the Commit button (✔) in the tool options bar to accept your editing changes.

Saving your work file

In this procedure, you'll save your work file so you can review it at a later time.

1 Choose File > Save. The Save As window opens.

2 Navigate to the My CIB Work folder.

3 In the Save As window enter the following settings:

• In File name, type **bride_work**.

• In Format, confirm that Photoshop (PSD) is selected.

4 Under Save Options, confirm that the Include in the Organizer option is selected and then deselect Save in Version Set with Original.

5 Review your settings and click the Save button. If the Photoshop Elements Format Options dialog box appears, keep Maximize Compatibility selected, and click OK.

6 Choose File > Close.

Congratulations, you've finished your first text project. In this section, you've formatted and edited the text, and seen how layers work independently in an image. You've also enlarged the canvas size without stretching the image itself.

Making cartoon balloons

Earlier in this lesson, you saw how text floated above the original photograph on its own layer. In this project, you'll go one step further and add an intermediate layer.

Your goal is one you've probably seen on humorous greeting cards, where the artist has combined a cartoon speech balloon with a photograph to put words in the mouth of the person or animal pictured. It's a fun thing to do with group photographs, or to tell a story in a lighthearted way. When we're finished, we'll have created a custom birthday card for a friend who's a drummer.

The original photograph (left) and finished project (right).

Opening the image file

You'll start by finding and opening the file, using Organizer tags.

1 If Photoshop Elements is open in Standard Edit mode, click Photo Browser on the shortcuts bar to switch to the Organizer.

2 If the Back to All Photos button appears above the thumbnails, click it now.

3 In the Tags palette, click the Find boxes for the Lesson 7 and Project 2 tags, so that the only thumbnail with both these tags appears.

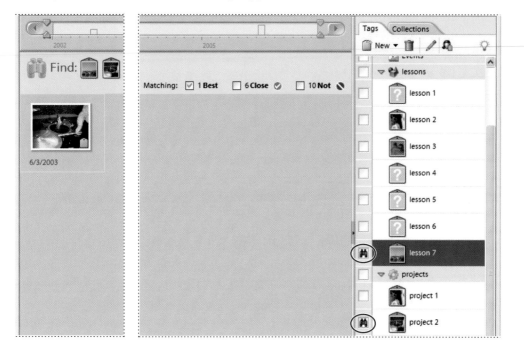

4 Click once to select the image thumbnail showing the picture of drums.

5 Click Edit (📷) on the shortcuts bar, and choose Go to Standard Edit.

Drawing a cartoon balloon in one stroke

In this exercise, you'll modify default tools and use a palette menu to change settings for each tool. Palette menus are available for some palettes, but not all. They provide additional commands and choices that apply to items shown in the palette.

1	In the toolbox, click and hold the Rectangle tool (☐) until a list appears showing all the shape tools. Select the Custom Shape tool.

Note: *Be careful not to confuse the Gradient tool (▨) or Rectangular Marquee tool (⬚) with the Rectangle tool.*

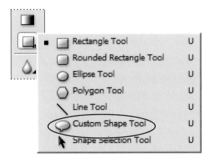

Notice that the Custom Shape tool replaces the Rectangle tool in the toolbox.

2	In the tool options bar, click the drop-down arrow located to the right of the word Shape to open the palette of custom shapes. In the custom shape palette that appears, click the arrow in the upper right corner of the palette. From the palette menu, choose Talk Bubbles.

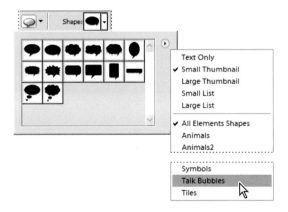

3	Double-click to select the Talk 1 shape.

The shape's name appears in a tooltip when you roll your cursor over it.

4   Click and drag diagonally inside the image to draw a balloon next to the drummer.

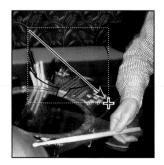

5   In the tool options bar, click the arrow to the right of the Color swatch and select the white swatch from the palette. Press Enter to close the palette.

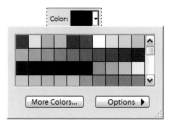

6   To have the talk balloon face the same direction as the drummer, you will flip the balloon's image. Select the Move tool. In the Layers palette, make sure the Shape 1 layer is selected and choose Image > Rotate > Flip Layer Horizontal; this flips the balloon so it is facing the drummer. As needed, make the following adjustments:

•   To move the balloon, move the cursor inside the shape and drag.

•   To resize the shape, drag the corners of the shape bounding box. You may need to check the Show Bounding Box checkbox in the tool options bar.

If you have made edits, and the Commit button (✔) appears on the tool options bar, click it, or press Enter.

Note: If you resize the shape, the Commit step is required for you to proceed. If you only move the shape, the Commit and Cancel buttons do not appear.

Adding text over the custom shape

In this procedure, you'll get a chance to practice the techniques for creating text that you used earlier in this lesson.

1   In the toolbox, select the Type tool (T).

2   In the tool options bar, select the following from the drop-down menus:

• For font family, select Arial.

• For font style, select Bold.

• For font size, type in **16 pt**.

Note: You're not limited to the preset sizes that are listed under the font size menu. You can type in any size in the font size field.

• For paragraph alignment, select Center Text (≡).

• For Color, confirm the color is set to black, or click the arrow to open the Color Swatches palette and select Black. Don't be concerned if the Color Swatches palette remains visible, as it will get closed in the next step.

3   Click to place a text insertion point near the top center of the balloon shape, and then type **Drummers keep the beat alive!**

4   Press Enter on the keyboard (not on the numeric keypad) twice to create two line breaks, and then type **Happy Birthday Larry**!

5   Using the same techniques you used in Project 1, edit the text as needed to correct any typing errors, and then click the Commit button (✔) in the tool options bar.

6   Using the Move tool (▶⊕), drag the text block to center it over the talk balloon shape.

When the Move tool is selected, you can use the arrow keys on your keyboard to move a layer in small increments instead of dragging it using your mouse. Similarly, you can use the arrow keys to move a selection when a selection tool is active.

Adding more custom shapes for decoration

There are more themes that are available than just the balloons. We'll add some more of these shapes to add a nice decorative touch geared toward music.

1   In the toolbox, select the Custom Shape tool (🗩).

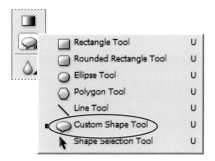

2   In the tool options bar, click the Shape drop-down arrow to open the palette of custom shapes. In the upper right corner of the custom shapes palette, click the arrow to open the palette menu, and choose Music.

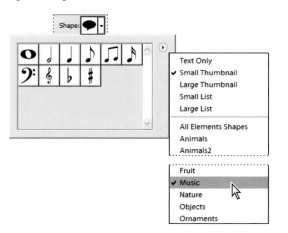

3   Double-click to select the treble clef shape (or choose another shape if you prefer).

4   In the tool options bar click the drop-down arrow to the right of the color swatch and click the RGB Green color swatch. Press Enter after choosing the color swatch.

5   Click and drag to draw the treble clef shape.

Note: *Holding down the Shift key as you draw a shape keeps the width and height proportional.*

6   After drawing the first shape, select the Move tool (▶⊕) and reposition, resize or rotate the shape as desired. After modifying the location or size of the shape, choose Select > Deselect Layers to commit the image and deselect the new shape layer.

7   To add more shapes (we added three more), repeat steps 2 through 6.

8   Choose File > Save. In the Save As dialog box, navigate to the My CIB Work folder, and name the file **drummer_work**. If Save in Version Set with Original is selected, be sure to deselect it before you click Save. If the Photoshop Elements Format Options dialog box appears, keep Maximize Compatibility selected, and click OK.

The file you've created now has multiple layers: the Background (the original photograph image), layers for each shape, and the text layer. Each layer can be changed independently of the others.

9   Choose File > Close. Be certain not to save any changes to the original photo.

Congratulations, you've finished another project. In the process, you've gained experience creating custom shape layers, adding text, and editing text.

Embossing text on an image

In the first two projects of this lesson, you've preserved the layering of the work files by saving in a file format that supports layers. This provides you with the flexibility to make changes to the images after they have been saved, without having to rebuild the image from the beginning, or modifying the original image. The layers have kept the text and shapes separate from the original image.

In this project, you'll add text to a photograph, creating a caption. You'll then save the photos in a format so they can be shared on a Web page.

Creating a new document for the text

You'll start by preparing the text in its own file.

1   In Photoshop Elements Editor, choose File > New > Blank File.

2   In the New dialog box, enter the following settings:

- For Name, type **Emboss_text**.
- For Width, type **640** and select pixels.
- For Height, type **425** and select pixels.
- For Resolution, type **72** and select pixels/inch.
- For Color Mode, select RGB Color.
- For Background Contents, select Transparent.
- Review your settings to make sure they are correct, and click OK.

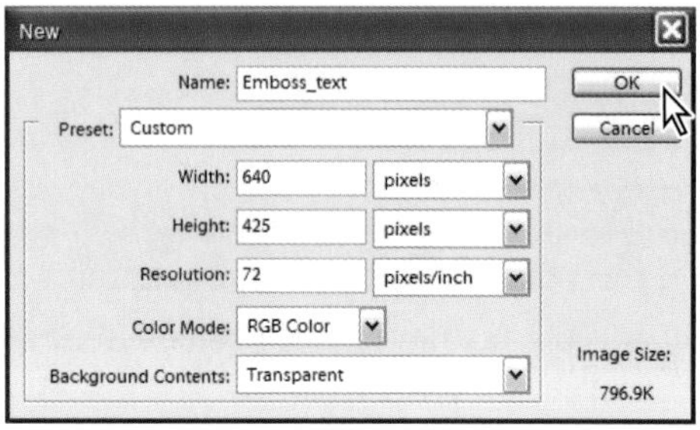

The image window shows only a checkerboard pattern. The pattern represents the transparent background that you selected when creating the file.

3   Select the Type tool (T).

4   In the tool options bar, set the following text attributes:

- Arial
- Bold
- 36 pt
- Left aligned
- Black

5   Click near the left side of the image window and type **Maine Vacation, July 2005**. Click the Commit button (✔) in the tool options bar to accept the text you've typed.

6   Select the Move tool (▶♣). Click and drag the text to center it in the image window.

7   Position the Move tool outside a corner of the text bounding box. The cursor changes to a curved, double-ended arrow (⌐). Drag left to rotate the text so it appears at a slight angle.

Note: You can also resize or reshape the text by dragging corners of the bounding box.

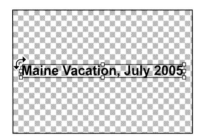

8   Click the Commit button (✔) on the tool options bar.

Photoshop Elements text layers are vector shapes. These shapes can be scaled and remain smooth even if they are resized.

Adding the text to multiple images

Now that you've prepared the text, you'll place it into your images.

1   Click Photo Browser (⊖▦) on the shortcuts bar to switch to the Organizer. If the Back to All Photos button appears above the thumbnails, select it now.

2   On the Tags palette, click the Find boxes for the Lesson 7 and Project 3 tags to find the thumbnails for the three images you'll use for this project: dock.jpg, boat.jpg, and coast.jpg.

3   Choose Edit > Select All, and then click Edit (◣) on the shortcuts bar. From the Edit drop-down menu, choose Go to Standard Edit.

4   On the right side of the menu bar, click the Tile button (⊞) to arrange the four open images in the work area.

💡 *You can also choose Window > Images > Tile to tile your images.*

5 In the Photo Bin (the row of thumbnails across the bottom of the work area), select the Emboss_text thumbnail to make it the active file.

6 In the Layers palette, hold down the Shift key, drag the layer thumbnail for the Maine Vacation text layer, and drop it in the picture of the boy on the dock.

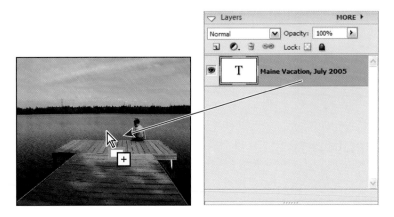

7 Repeat the previous step, dragging the text into the boat.jpg and coast.jpg images.

8 In the Editor window, click to select the document containing only the text. Choose File > Close. When asked to Save, click Yes, then enter the name **Emboss_text** and save the file as a Photoshop (PSD) format in the My CIB Work folder on your hard disk. If the Photoshop Elements Format Options dialog box appears, keep Maximize Compatibility selected, and click OK.

Applying the embossing effect to the text layer

Next you'll work with an effect. Effects are combinations of adjustments that you apply in one easy action. Because these adjustments are art attributes instead of font attributes, the text layer must be simplified before you can apply the effect.

1 On the right side of the menu bar, click the Cascade Windows button, or choose Window > Images > Cascade.

2 In the Photo Bin, select the dock.jpg thumbnail—the picture of the boy on the dock—to make the image active. Select the text layer in the Layers palette.

3 In the Palette Bin locate the Styles and Effects palette. If necessary, click the triangle in the upper left corner of the Styles and Effects palette to expand it. If the palette is not displayed in your work area, choose Window > Styles and Effects.

4   At the top of the Styles and Effects palette, select Effects from the drop-down menu on the left side and choose text effects from the drop-down menu on the right side.

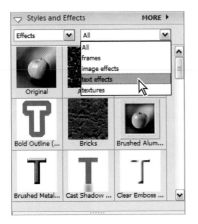

5   Double-click the Clear Emboss effect thumbnail to apply it to the selected text layer.

In the Layers palette, the Maine Vacation text layer thumbnail icon no longer displays the T icon for text. When the effect was applied, it converted the text layer into a locked layer. You should make all text editing changes before applying effects to text layers.

6   Repeat Steps 2 through 5 to apply the Clear Emboss effect to the text layers in the boat.jpg and the coast.jpg files.

Saving copies of the images for Web use

Your final task for this project is to convert the files to JPEG format so they can be shared on an Web page. The JPEG file format reduces the file size and can be displayed by Web browsers such as Internet Explorer, which makes it an efficient file format for Web use. The conversion to the JPEG file format also flattens each image file so that the words and the original image are merged into one inseparable layer.

Here you'll use the Save for Web feature, which allows you to compare the original image file with the proposed Web version of the image.

1   In the Photo Bin, select the dock.jpg thumbnail, and choose File > Save for Web.

2   Under the two views of the image, notice the file-size information. The image on the left displays the file size of the original Photoshop document.

Note: When previewing images using Save for Web, you can use the Zoom tool (🔍) in the upper left corner of the dialog box to zoom in, or (by holding down Alt and clicking) zoom out. Use the Hand tool (✋) to drag both images at once, so that you see the same details in both views.

3 On the right side of the dialog box, select JPEG Medium in the Preset drop-down menu.

Notice the change in the file size for the JPEG image on the right side of the window.

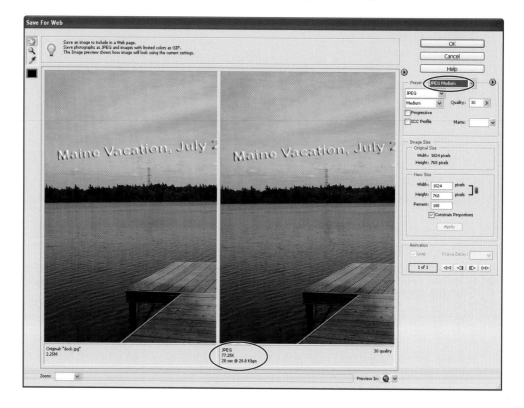

4 Under New Size, select Constrain Proportions, and type **480** in the Width field.

Because you selected Constrain Proportions, the Height automatically changes to keep the image proportional.

5 In the New Size section of the Save for Web window, click the Apply button. Again notice the file size displayed beneath the JPEG view of the image.

Note: If you need to reduce the file size even more, you can select JPEG Low, which reduces the file size by discarding more image data and further compressing the image. You can select intermediate levels between these options by changing the Quality value, either by typing a different number or by clicking the arrow and dragging the slider.

6   Click OK, and the Save Optimized As window opens.

7   If necessary, navigate to the My CIB Work folder and then add -**final** to the end of the file name. Click Save.

8   Repeat Steps 1-6 for the other two image files, saving the files as boat-final.jpg and coast-final.jpg.

Converting the files to the JPEG format reduces the file size by using JPEG compression, and discarding some of the data based upon the setting you select.

9   Back in the Editor, choose File > Save. Add -**work** to the file name so the original file is not modified. Save the file in the Photoshop (PSD) format to the My CIB Work folder. If the Photoshop Elements Format Options dialog box appears, keep Maximize Compatibility selected, and click OK.

10   Choose File > Close.

11   Repeat steps 9 and 10 for the two remaining images.

Congratulations! You've completed this project. You'll want to close any files that remain open. In this project, you created a new Photoshop (PSD) format document and added text to the blank document. You then copied a text layer from one document to another image file. You also used the Styles and Effects palette to apply an effect to a text layer.

Using Creations, Layer Styles, and distortions

One of the concepts introduced in the previous project was simplifying a text layer—converting it to art so that you could apply artistic effects to the character shapes. After you simplified the text, you could no longer edit the text with the Type tool.

While certain effects do require that the text be simplified before they can be applied to the text, there are many other text effects that can be applied to text that remains fully editable. In this project you'll use Creations to build the foundation of your project. You will then modify the text and create a text title on top of an image, building the photo into the title page of a calendar project.

Adding the subject text

Your first task is to find and open the image file for this project and add the text.

1   Click Photo Browser ( ) to switch to the Organizer. If the Back to All Photos button appears above the thumbnails, select it now.

2   On the Tags palette, click the Find boxes for the Lesson 7 and Project 4 tags to find the image thumbnail for this project—the boys swimming.

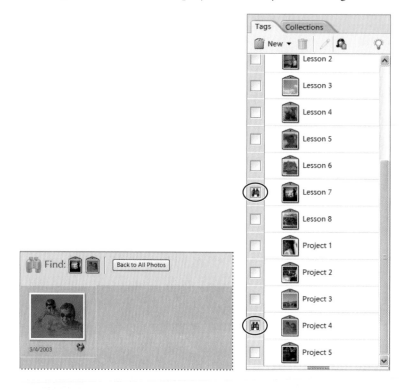

3   Select the thumbnail. Then click Edit ( ) in the shortcuts bar, and choose Go to Standard Edit from the drop-down menu.

4   In the toolbox, select the Type tool (T) and make the following selections in the
tool options bar to set the text attributes:

• For the font family, select Arial or Arial Black.

• For the font style, select Bold, if it is available.

• For the font size, type **130 pt** Press Enter to accept this setting.

• For text alignment, select Center text ( ).

• For leading ( ), type **112 pt**.

• Set the text color to black.

5   Using the Type tool, click near the center of the image. Type the word **SUMMER**
and press the Enter key and then type **FUN!** on the second line.

Note: Do not use the Enter key from the numeric keypad.

6   Click the Commit button (✔) in the tool options bar to accept the text.

7   Choose the Move tool (▶⊹). Click and drag the text to the bottom left corner of the
picture.

Warping text

Stretching and skewing text into unusual shapes is incredibly easy in Photoshop
Elements 4.0. Make sure that the Type tool (T) is selected before you begin.

1   In the image window, click on the words SUMMER FUN! using the Type tool.

Note: It isn't necessary to highlight the text because warping applies to the entire text layer.

2   On the tool options bar, click Create warped text ( ), which opens the Warp Text
dialog box.

3 In the Style drop-down menu, select Flag. Confirm that Horizontal is chosen for the orientation of the effect and set the Bend value to +22. Click OK to close the dialog box.

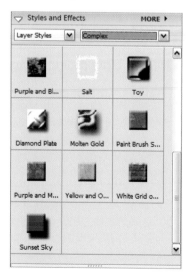

4 Click the Commit button (✔) in the tool options bar.

Stylizing and editing the text

Earlier, you applied an Effect to text, which required you to simplify the text in the process. In this procedure, you'll use the Styles and Effects palette again, but this time you'll apply a Layer Style instead of an Effect. Layer Styles don't require simplified text, so the text remains editable.

1 In the Layers palette, make sure that the SUMMER FUN! text layer is still selected, or select it now. If the Commit button (✔) still appears in the tool options bar, select it.

2 In the Styles and Effects palette, choose Layer Styles from the drop-down menu on the left side of the palette and choose Complex from the drop-down menu on the right side of the palette.

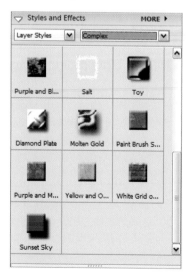

3   Scroll down through the palette to the last thumbnail, Sunset Sky. Double-click the Sunset Sky effect to apply it to the selected layer, SUMMER FUN!

The Layer Style gives the text color, and adds a bevel and a drop shadow, giving the text a raised, three-dimensional look.

4   Using the Type tool (T), click between the word FUN and the exclamation point so you can add the year to the photo.

Note: If you have trouble with this step, make sure that the Type tool is selected in the toolbox and the SUMMER FUN! layer is selected in the Layers palette. Then try again.

5   Press the Enter key to break the line, and type to add the year, **2005**. Then click the Commit button (✔) on the tool options bar. Use the Move tool (▶⊕) to move the type layer up and into view.

Even after applying dramatic changes to the appearance of the text, you can still make edits. This provides flexibility to make editorial changes to your work files even after the text has been stylized.

Creating an unstylized copy of the text layer

You will create two versions of the finished artwork and create these versions on separate layers of the same work file, instead of creating two work files.

1   In the Layers palette, select the text layer. Then click the More menu in the upper right corner of the palette. The palette menu is displayed. From the palette menu, choose Duplicate Layer. Click OK to accept the default layer name.

💡 *You can also drag an existing layer to the New Layer icon (⬜) in the Layers palette to create a duplicate layer.*

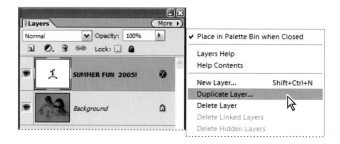

2   Click the eye icon (👁) to the left of the original SUMMER FUN 2005! layer. The layer becomes invisible in the image window.

Because there are two identical text layers that are perfectly aligned, you will not notice any difference in the image window.

3   In the Layers palette, make sure the SUMMER FUN 2005! copy layer is selected and choose Layer > Layer Style > Clear Layer Style.

The warped text now appears in solid black, as it did before you applied the Layer Style.

Simplifying and applying a pattern to text

You're now ready to add a different look to the copy of the text layer. Make sure that the SUMMER FUN 2005! copy layer is selected in the Layers palette before you begin.

One of the interesting things you'll do in this procedure is to lock the transparent pixels on a text layer. This enables you to do all sorts of painting on the shapes in the layer without having to be careful to avoid the edges.

1   Using the Type tool, drag to select all the black SUMMER FUN 2005! text.

💡 *You can also select all the text by clicking to create an insertion point in the text and choosing Select > All.*

2   In the tool options bar, click the arrow to the right of the Color swatch to open the Color Swatches palette. Click the White swatch to select White as the text color. Press the Enter key to close the palette.

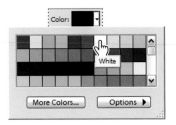

3   In the toolbox, choose the Clone Stamp tool. In the tool options bar, choose the Pattern Stamp tool icon (📌).

Note: *You can also choose the Pattern Stamp tool by pressing and holding the Clone Stamp tool in the toolbar.*

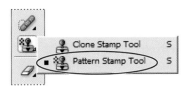

4   In the tool options bar, select the following:

•   For Size, enter **100** px. This sets the diameter of the Pattern Stamp tool brush, and can be set by typing, or by clicking the arrow to the right of the value and dragging the slider to change the size.

•   For Mode, confirm that Normal is selected.

•   For Opacity, confirm that 100% is selected.

- Make sure that the Bubbles pattern is selected. Bubbles is the default pattern.

Note: If you do not see the Bubbles thumbnail, click the arrow to open the Pattern Picker, choose either Default or Patterns in the palette menu, and then double-click the Bubbles thumbnail to select it and close the palette.

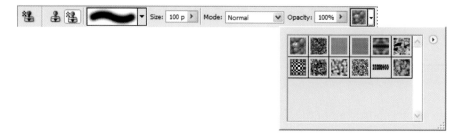

5   Click with the Pattern Stamp brush on the SUMMER FUN 2005! text. When a message appears, asking if you want to simplify the layer, click OK. After clicking OK, do not click on the text again.

6   In the Layers palette, click the Lock Transparent Pixels button to prevent changes to the transparent areas of the simplified SUMMER FUN 2005! layer.

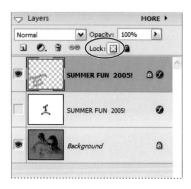

Notice that there is now a lock icon on the upper SUMMER FUN 2005! layer, reminding you that you've applied a lock.

7   Paint with the Pattern Stamp tool, applying the pattern as solidly or unevenly as you like. Once you're finished painting the image, you'll add a drop shadow to the text.

8 In the Styles and Effects palette, make sure that Layer Styles is still selected in the drop-down menu on the left side. In the drop-down menu on the right side, choose Drop Shadows. Confirm that the topmost SUMMER FUN 2005! layer is selected, and double-click the Soft Edge drop shadow to apply the effect.

The pattern affects only the selected layer (the simplified text) and doesn't change any unselected layer, such as the underlying photograph. Because the transparent pixels on the upper SUMMER FUN 2005! layer are locked, they are also protected, so only the simplified text shapes take on the pattern.

Simplifying the text layer, as you've done here, makes it unable to be edited with the Type tool. However, you can add dimension to the patterned text by applying a Layer Style, such as a Bevel or Inner Glow, using the Styles and Effects palette.

Hiding and revealing layers to review the two versions

You'll use the eye icons in the Layers palette to alternately show and hide the two layers with the SUMMER FUN 2005! message.

1   In the Layers palette, make sure that the eye icons appear in the Layers palette for the Background layer and the upper SUMMER FUN 2005! layer that you just painted with the Pattern Stamp tool.

2   Click the eye icon for the top layer, SUMMER FUN 2005! This hides the layer and the eye icon is no longer displayed.

3   Click the empty box to the left of the middle SUMMER FUN 2005! layer. This causes the eye icon to display and also displays the text layer with the Sunset Sky layer style.

4   Change the visibility back and forth between the two layers until you decide which one you like better. Leave that layer showing and hide the other SUMMER FUN 2005! layer.

5   Choose File > Save, and save the file as 07_04_Work in the My CIB Work folder. Choose PSD as the format. If Save in Version Set with Original is selected, be sure to deselect it before you click Save. If the Photoshop Elements Format Options dialog box appears, keep Maximize Compatibility selected, and click OK.

Now that the file is saved, you'll add it as the title page to a calendar project using Creations

6   If you are still in the Editor, click the Photo Browser button to switch to the Organizer and in the Organizer click the Back to All Photos button if it is visible.

7   In the Organizer, choose File > Create > Calendar Pages… The Create Calendar window opens.

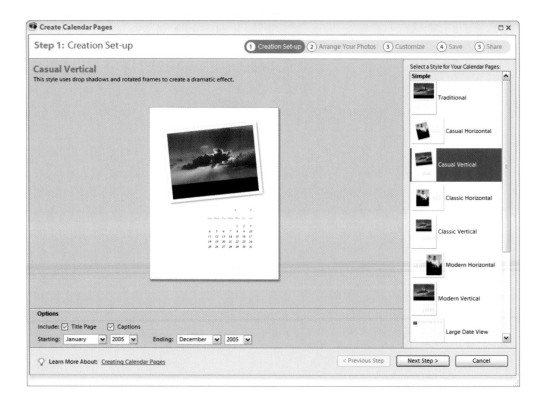

8   In the Step 1 window, choose Casual Vertical from the list on the right and set the starting and ending dates for the calendar in the bottom left corner of the window, then click the Next Step button.

9   In the Step 2 window, click the Add Photos button. In the Add Photos window, click Entire Catalog to display all photos in the current catalog. Choose 13 images so that you have an image for each month and an image for the cover of the calendar. Click Add Selected Photos. Click the Done button in the Add Photos window.

Note: *If any of the images you select are low resolution, and do not contain enough information to print, you will receive a warning message. Click OK to close the alert.*

10   Confirm the arrangement of the images and click the Next Step button.

11   In the Step 3 window, double-click the title page text and enter **Smith Family Calendar 2006**. Click Done. Click the Next Step button.

12   In the Step 4 window, enter a name for the calendar in the upper right corner of the window and click the Save button.

13   In the Step 5 window, determine the method you would like to use for sharing the calendar and click the appropriate button to print, create a PDF, or send the calendar by e-mail. To not print or share the calendar click Done. The calendar is saved in the Organizer so you can easily access it in the future.

In this project, you've applied a Layer Style to text that you warped. You've learned how to create duplicate layers and how to remove a Layer Style. You've seen how locking transparent pixels on a layer helps you preserve the margins of the visible areas. Finally, you've kept two potential versions of the final art in one work file and used the Creation feature to build a calendar.

Using Layer Styles and creating an animation

In this exercise, you're going to create a simple animation that will act as a graphic for the first page of a Web gallery.

While the focus of this project is on text, animations can include graphic files without text. As you become more comfortable with building animations, you can add frames to make the changes more gradual or include additional content. You can create an animation that plays only once or one that loops endlessly as long as the file is open.

Original.   Animation frame 1.   Animation frame 2.

Setting up layers for the project

In the Layers palette, a lock icon appears on the Background layer and the word Background is shown in italics. That's because the Background layer carries certain limitations on what you can do to it.

In this project, you'll want to make some changes that are not possible without unlocking the Background layer. As you saw in the previous project, you lock or unlock an ordinary layer by selecting it and then selecting the lock icon at the top of the Layers palette. While this doesn't work with the Background layer, you will unlock it by changing its name.

1   Using the techniques you've used in the other projects in this chapter, switch to the Organizer and click to find the Lesson 7 and Project 5 tags. In the Organizer, select and open the sunset.jpg file in Standard Edit.

2   In the Layers palette, click the Background layer and then choose Layer > Duplicate Layer. Click OK to accept the default layer name.

Two layers are now visible in the Layers palette: Background and Background copy. Only the Background layer displays the lock icon (🔒).

3   Double-click the Background layer to open the New Layer dialog box. Click OK to accept the default name, Layer 0.

The lock no longer appears on Layer 0, which was previously the Background layer.

You're going to use these two editable copies of the original layer. They will serve as the foundation for the two-frame animation.

Adding and arranging text layers

The process of adding and duplicating text layers is practically old hat to you at this stage of the lesson. In this procedure, you'll do something new: rearrange the stacking order of the layers.

1   In the Layers palette, select the Background copy layer.

2   Select the Type tool (T), and use the tool options bar to select Arial Black. Set the size to 280 pt, and press Enter to accept the size change. Set the Leading (⚐) to Auto, and Left align (≡) the text. If Arial Black is not available on your computer, you can choose Arial or Helvetica and select the Bold option.

3   Click near the bottom of the image, type **My Web**, press Enter to break the line, and type **Gallery**. For our example, we typed Sean's Web Gallery. Click the Commit button (✔) on the tool options bar or press Enter on the numeric keypad to accept the typing.

4 Select the Move tool (🛦⁺) and drag the text as needed to center it at the bottom of the image window.

5 In the Layers palette, drag the Web Gallery text layer to the New Layer icon to create a copy of the text layer, which will be labeled Web Gallery copy.

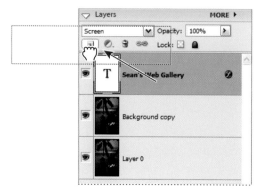

6 In the Layers palette, select the Background copy layer and drag it upwards into position between the two text layers—the Web Gallery and the Web Gallery copy layers.

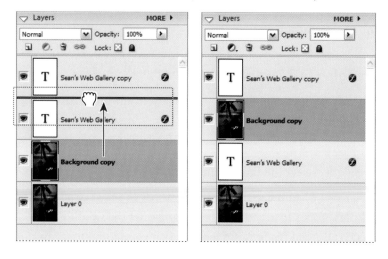

Adding neon effects to text

Your Layers palette is set up with alternating versions of the sunset image and the Web Gallery text. So far, this doesn't seem too practical, because all you can see are the upper text layer and Background copy, which block your view of the lower text layer and Layer 0.

In this procedure, you'll apply Layer Styles that give the two text layers very different appearances.

1   In the Layers palette, select the upper text layer, which is the Web Gallery copy.

2   In the Styles and Effects palette, choose Layer Styles from the drop-down menu on the left side of the palette and choose Wow Neon from the drop-down menu on the right side of the palette.

3   Scroll to locate the Wow-Neon Dk Blue Off effect in the palette. Click the Wow-Neon Dk Blue Off thumbnail once to apply it to the copy of the text layer.

Note: Be sure to select the Off version of the Wow-Neon Dk Blue layer style. If you can't read the whole Layer Style name, let the cursor hover over a thumbnail until a tool tip appears identifying it. Or click More at the top of the palette to open the palette menu, and select List View to change how the effects are displayed in the palette.

4   In the Layers palette, click the eye icons (👁) for the Web Gallery copy layer and the Background copy layer to hide them in the image window.

5   Select the Web Gallery text layer.

6   In the Styles and Effects palette, do the following:

•   Click the Wow-Neon Red On thumbnail to apply it to the selected layer, Web Gallery.

•   Click the Wow-Neon Red Off thumbnail to also apply it to the Web Gallery layer.

Adding a second Layer Style does not replace the first style. It enhances the initial style.

Merging layers in preparation for animating

Although the text looks like art, it's not. It can still be edited using the Type tool. For example, you could use the Type tool to change the word from Gallery to Photos on the individual layers. But that flexibility will end during this procedure.

Because of this, it's a good idea to create a copy—just in case you might need to change the file later and don't want to have to start again from the beginning.

1   Choose File > Save As, and use the Save As dialog box to name the file **07_05_Work**. Choose PSD as the format. Save it in the My CIB Work folder. If Save in Version Set with Original is selected, be sure to deselect it before you click Save. If the Photoshop Elements Format Options dialog box appears, keep Maximize Compatibility selected, and click OK.

2   Choose File > Duplicate, and type **07_05_Merged** in the Duplicate Image dialog box. Click OK and a duplicate of the file appears. This allows you to maintain a copy of the file with layers that can be edited, while working on a duplicate version in which you will merge the layers together. Close the original work file.

3   In the Layers palette, click to make the eye icons (👁) visible for the Web Gallery copy and Background copy layers, making the layers visible again, and then select the Web Gallery copy layer.

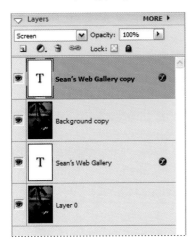

4   Choose Layer > Merge Down to flatten the Web Gallery copy and Background copy layer into one merged layer.

Note: If the Merge Down command is unavailable (dimmed), make sure that you have the Web Gallery copy layer selected in the Layers palette and that both the Web Gallery copy and Background copy layers have eye icons in the Layers palette. Then try again.

5   Select the Web Gallery layer in the Layers palette, and again choose Layer > Merge Down to flatten the text layer with Layer 0.

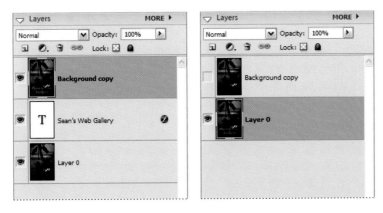

6   Choose File > Save. Then click Save in the Save As dialog box without making any further changes. If the Photoshop Elements Format Options dialog box appears, keep Maximize Compatibility selected, and click OK.

This process reduces the file to two layers, one with blue neon Web Gallery text superimposed on the sunset image and one with glowing red neon Web Gallery text on the same sunset image. You can see the two layers by clicking the eye icon for the upper layer off and on to show it or hide it, revealing the lower layer.

Animating the two layers

You've actually completed the most difficult phases of this project. Now here comes the fun part: creating the animation. First, we'll have to reduce the image size of the file.

1   With the 07_05_Merged file still active, make sure that both the Background copy and Layer 0 layers are visible, or click the eye icons (👁) for the layers to make the layers visible. Then, choose Image > Resize > Image Size… Select the Resample Image checkbox at the bottom left corner of the window, and for the Pixel Dimension width, enter **320** with the units set to pixels. Click OK to resize the image.

2   Choose File > Save for Web.

3   In the Preset drop-down menu, choose GIF 128 No Dither. Then click in the Animate checkbox.

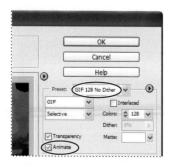

4   Under Animation, select Loop, and select 1.0 seconds in the Frame Delay drop-down menu. If the Animation options are not available, make sure that you selected Animate in the Preset area of the dialog box in the previous step.

5 In the New Size area, make sure the image size is 320 pixels wide and 480 pixels high. If they are correct, go to the next step. If the image size is incorrect, do all of the following in this order:

• Select Constrain Proportions.

• In Width, type **320** pixels.

• Click Apply, and notice the reduced file size and download times listed under the optimized version of the image.

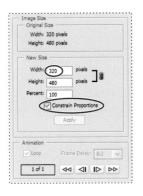

Note: After you click Apply, you can't modify this change. If you decide that the file size and quality are too low, click Cancel to close the Save for Web dialog box and start again.

6 Review all settings, and click OK. In the Save Optimized As dialog box, type **intro_animation** as the file name, and click Save to save it in the My CIB Work folder.

7 Save and close the 07_05_Merged file. In Windows Explorer, locate the intro_anim. gif file and double-click on it.

The animation opens in your default application for viewing .gif files, such as Windows Picture and Fax Viewer or your Web browser. When you finish enjoying your animation, close the viewer and return to Photoshop Elements.

You've completed the final project in Lesson 7. In this project, you've dragged layers to change the stacking order in the Layers palette. You've unlocked the Background layer by changing its name. You've applied multiple Layer Styles to different layers, and you've merged two layers into one—twice! Finally, you've explored one of the many uses of the Save for Web dialog box.

Review

▶ **Review questions**

1   What is the advantage of having text on a separate layer?

2   How do you hide a layer without removing it?

3   In the Layers palette, what do the lock icons do and how do they work?

▶ **Review answers**

1   Because the text remains separate from the image, Photoshop Elements text layers can be edited in later work sessions, just like most other kinds of text documents.

2   You can hide a layer by clicking the eye icon next to that layer on the Layers palette. To make the layer visible again, click the empty box where the eye icon should be to restore it.

3   Lock icons prevent changes to a layer. You can click Lock All to lock all the pixels on the selected layer, or you can click Lock Transparent Pixels to protect specific areas. To remove a lock, select the locked layer and click the active lock icon to toggle it off. (This does not work for the Background layer, which can be unlocked only by renaming and converting it into an ordinary layer.)

8 | Combining Multiple Images

Sometimes you may want to merge various images—whether to add an effect, or move a person or object from one photo into another.

In this lesson you will do the following:

- Copy and paste selected areas of one image into another.

- Resize the canvas area of an image.

- Define and use a specific width-height ratio for cropping.

- Scale a layer.

- Create a gradient from opaque to transparent.

- Apply a clipping path to an image layer.

- Paint on a layer.

This lesson includes four independent projects. You'll need approximately 90 minutes to complete them all.

In this lesson, you will use the CIB Catalog you created earlier in the book. If necessary, open this catalog by choosing File > Catalog in Organizer mode, then click Open.

Getting started

1 Start Photoshop Elements 4.0 Editor in Standard Edit mode. If you are in the Organizer, choose Edit > Go to Standard Edit to open the Editor.

2 Open the Palette and Photo Bins, if they are not already open, by clicking the arrows (▮▶) and (▼) at the bottom of the work area or by choosing Window > Palette Bin, and Window > Photo Bin.

3   Review the contents of the Palette Bin, making sure that the Layers, Navigator, Styles and Effects, and Undo History palettes are displayed.

Note: For help with Palette Bin contents, see "Using the Palette Bin" in Lesson 3.

Copying from one image into another

A simple way to combine part of one image with another is to use the familiar Copy and Paste commands. Your goal in this project is to enhance a street corner in San Francisco's Chinatown.

1   Click on the Photo Browser button to enter Organizer mode. Then select the 08_01a, 08_01b, and 08_01c files—three photos of San Francisco's Chinatown. Choose Edit > Go to Standard Edit to open these files in the Editor.

2   Select the 08_01b thumbnail in the Photo Bin to make it active, and then select the Lasso tool (𝒫) in the toolbox.

3   Drag the Lasso tool around the dragon statue image. Keep the selection reasonably close to the outer edge of the dragon, but you don't have to be precise.

If necessary, you can select Add to Selection (⧉) or Subtract from Selection (⧉) in the tool options bar, and then drag around the small areas you want to add or subtract from the first selection.

4   Choose Edit > Copy, or press Ctrl+C.

5   Select the 08_01a thumbnail in the Photo Bin to make that image active. Choose Edit > Paste, or press Ctrl+V. This places the copied image into the 08_01a picture.

6   Use the Move tool (✣) to resize and move the pasted-in layer so that it fits in the scene. When it looks right to you, click the Commit button (✔) in the tool options bar.

7   Select the 08_01c thumbnail in the Photo Bin, and repeat Steps 3-6 to add the street sign to the 08_01a picture.

💡 *To duplicate the pasted object, hold down the Alt key and drag with the Move tool. This duplicates and moves the selection.*

8   Save your work by choosing File > Save. For format choose Photoshop (PSD) and for a file name type **08_01_Work**. For location, choose the My CIB Work folder you created in the beginning of the book. If the Photoshop Elements Format Options dialog box appears, keep Maximize Compatibility selected, and click OK.

You're finished with this project, so you can close all the files without saving other changes. You can use the skills you've learned in previous lessons to remove any background behind the statue using the Magic Selection Brush or Selection Brush. Because the statue is on its own layer, you will erase the background behind the statue, not the scene into which it has been pasted.

Placing multiple photographs in one file

Sometimes you want to show several photographs side-by-side in a single image file. In this project, the photographs you'll use show different scenes of a tea house in San Francisco.

Cropping to synchronize the dimensions

Here you'll work with two images that have the same resolution and widths, but their heights are different because the images came from different sources.

When combining images of different sizes, you have three choices:

- Leave the images sized as they are;
- Crop the larger photograph to match the height of the first image; or
- Resize the larger photograph to match the height of the first image, but not its width.

In this procedure, you'll use the second method.

1   In the Organizer, select 08_02a and 08_02b and open them both in Standard Edit.

2   Select the Crop tool (⛏) in the toolbox.

3   In the tool options bar, type **428 px** (include the units) in Width and **640 px** in Height.

Note: The default units for Width and Height are inches, so it's important to include the px with the values.

4   In the image window for 08_02b, drag the Crop tool diagonally across the image, centering the bridge in the crop area.

5   Drag the handles at the corners as needed to include as much of the picture as possible. Be careful to keep the crop boundary within the image area.

Regardless of how you drag the corners, the proportions of the crop area remain constant because you set the relationship between width and height in Step 3.

6   Apply the crop in either of the following ways:

• Double-click in the image window.

• Click the Commit button (✔).

7   Click the Aspect Ratio drop-down menu in the options bar and choose No Restriction to clear the 428 by 640 width-to-height ratio you defined in Step 3.

Note: Until you click No Restriction, the aspect ratio will remain, regardless of which image file is active.

Combining pictures and resizing the canvas

Now that the pictures are equally sized, you can proceed to place both images in one file.

1   Arrange the two image windows so that you can see some portion of both images.

2   Select the Move tool (▶⊕).

3   Hold down the Shift key and drag the bridge photograph (08_02b) into the image window of the tea house photograph (08_02a). Carefully release the mouse button first and then release the Shift key. You can close the 08_02b (bridge) file now without saving any changes to the file.

As you can see in the Layers palette, the photographs are now stacked in separate layers. Only Layer 1 is visible: the picture of the bridge.

4   Choose Image > Resize > Canvas Size.

5   In the Canvas Size dialog box, do the following:

- For Anchor, select the middle square in the left column.

- Select the Relative check box.

- In Width, type **100** and select percent.

- Click OK.

Canvas Size

Learn more about: Canvas Size

OK

Cancel

Current Size: 800.6K
Width: 5.931 inches
Height 8.889 inches

New Size: 1.56M
Width: 100   percent
Height 0   percent
☑ Relative
Anchor:

Canvas extension color: Background

6   Hold down the Shift key and drag Layer 1, the bridge, to the right until its edges align with the far edges of the canvas. Holding down the Shift key as you drag constrains the movement so that the vertical position of the layer can't change. You may need to zoom out first before moving the image.

7   Choose File > Save As. Name the image 08_02_Work, and save it using the Photoshop (PSD) format in the My CIB Work folder. If the Photoshop Elements Format Options dialog box appears, keep Maximize Compatibility selected, and click OK. Close the file.

Erasing areas of image layers

In this project, you'll start with a Photoshop PSD file that we've prepared for you. In it, four photographs have been stacked in layers, each one blocking your view of the ones below it. This is similar to the two images you combined in the previous exercise. You will erase a portion of each layer, allowing parts of the other layers to show through. You'll end up with a collage, piecing together four city scenes into an equally divided image.

There are several ways to erase. One way is to use the Eraser tool, which replaces erased areas with the Background Color, just like a regular eraser removes pencil marks so that you can see the paper underneath. Another way is to use the Background Eraser tool, which replaces the erased area with transparent pixels, just like wiping wet paint off a piece of glass. In either case, the process involves dragging the eraser over the area you want to remove.

In this project, you'll erase by selecting and then deleting entire areas of the various layers. This makes it easy to create sharp, precise boundaries between the four quarters of the final image.

Setting up a grid for precise selections

Knowing how to use rulers and grids is essential when you do precision work.

1   Using the Organizer, open the 08_03.psd file (Coit Tower) in Standard Edit mode.

2   Choose View > Rulers, and then choose View > Grid.

3   On the View menu, make sure that there is a check mark by the Snap to Grid command, or choose that command now.

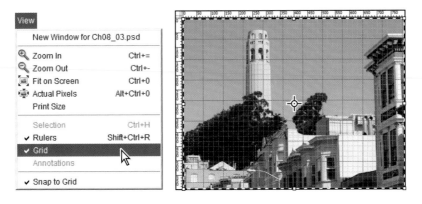

4   Choose Edit > Preferences > Grid, and then select the following:

- In Gridline Every, type **100** and select Pixels in the drop-down menu.

- In Subdivisions, type **4**, if it is not already entered.

- Click OK to close the Preferences dialog box.

5   In the image window, drag the zero-point marker (the corner box where the two rulers intersect) to the center of the image, so that it snaps into place at the center point of both rulers.

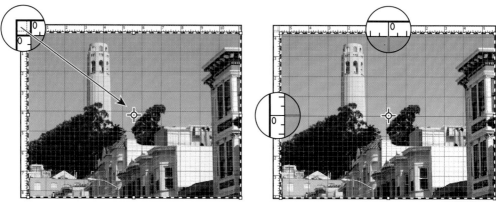

Before dragging the zero-point marker.   *After dragging the zero-point marker.*

Now the 0, 0 position on the rulers is set at the center of the image.

6   Choose File > Save As. Name the file **08_03_Work.psd**, and save it in the My CIB Work folder. If the Photoshop Elements Format Options dialog box appears, keep Maximize Compatibility selected, and click OK.

Erasing part of the top layer

This PSD file has four layers, which we created for you by dragging layers from several images into one file. Because the top layer covers the entire image area, all you can see is that layer—unless, of course, you peek at the Layers palette, where you can see thumbnails of all four layers.

1   In the Layers palette, select the top layer, Coit Tower, showing the tower.

Make sure the eye icon is visible for all the layers underneath the first layer. As each section is deleted, the layer underneath is exposed.

2   In the toolbox, select the Rectangular Marquee tool ( ).

3   Drag from the center of the image (0,0 point) to the upper left until the selection marquee snaps into place at the corner of the image.

4   Choose Select > Inverse to invert the selection.

Now everything except the first quadrant of the image is selected, and the upper left quadrant is protected from changing.

5   Choose Edit > Delete or press the Delete key on your keyboard.

Keep the selection active.

Erasing parts of lower layers in the image

By erasing three-quarters of the Coit Tower layer, you exposed three-quarters of the cable car layer, which is the the next layer down. You'll uncover parts of the bridge and arboretum layers by deleting portions of the other layers.

Before you begin, make sure that the selection from the previous procedure is still active and that the Rectangular Marquee tool (⬚) is selected.

1   In the Layers palette, click the eye icon (👁) for the Coit Tower layer to hide it, and select the cable car layer.

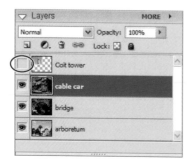

Note: It's not absolutely necessary to hide the layer, but it simplifies your view as you perform the next steps.

2   Choose Select > Inverse, so that only the upper left quadrant is selected. Then move the cursor inside the selection and drag it down till it snaps to the lower left corner of the image window.

Note: The shortcut for inverting a selection is Ctrl+Shift+I. You're going to invert numerous times in these steps, so this is a good chance to practice using it.

3   Invert the selection by choosing Select > Inverse or press Ctrl+Shift+I to select three-quarters of the cable car image. Press Delete or choose Edit > Delete, revealing three-quarters of the underlying bridge.

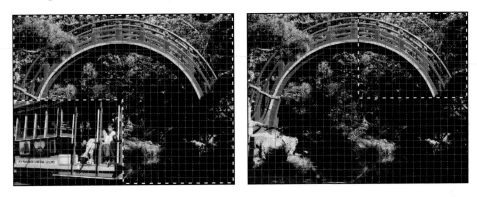

4   In the Layers palette, click the eye icon to hide the cable car layer.

5   Repeat the process to erase all but the top right quadrant of the bridge layer:

• Select the bridge layer.

• Invert the selection and drag it to the upper right quadrant. Then invert the selection again.

• Press Delete.

• Click the eye icon to hide the bridge layer.

6   Repeat the process to erase all but the lower right quadrant and reveal the arboretum image:

• Select the arboretum layer.

• Invert the selection and drag it to the lower right quadrant. Then invert the selection again.

• Press Delete.

7   Choose Select > Deselect.

8   Choose View > Snap to Grid, to deselect that option.

Note: The Snap to Grid feature can interfere with other kinds of work, especially when you try to select areas that don't align to the grid.

Finishing and saving the project

You've done your erasing. It's time to see the overall results. You're also going to save your work twice: one work file and one JPEG file.

1   Choose View > Rulers and then View > Grid, to turn off these displays.

2   In the Layers palette, click to restore the eye icons (👁) for each of the four layers so that all are visible.

Because you've used the Snap to Grid feature and rulers to align your selections precisely, your final image has no gaps between the quadrants or uneven margins.

3   Choose File > Save. (This saves the latest changes to the 08_03_Work.psd file in the My CIB Work folder.)

4   Choose File > Save As.

5   In the Save As dialog box, select JPEG as the format, and click Save. It is not necessary to change the file name or location.

6   In the JPEG Options dialog box, drag the Quality slider to 12. Notice the file-size information, then click OK.

7   Choose File > Close or click Close to close the file.

The JPEG format does not support layers, so creating a JPEG version of the image merges the layers into a single, flat image. JPEG is a good option for sharing files, as many programs and computer platforms support the format.

Congratulations! You've finished this project.

Now that you're done, can you think of another way to do this project? If you thought of the Cookie Cutter tool, you're right. It has a square shape option that you could use with the grid and rulers to cut out the quadrants directly rather than by inverting selections and deleting. For another example of using the Cookie Cutter, see Lesson 9, "Advanced Editing Techniques."

Using a gradient clipping path

Digital graphics work consistently challenges you to strike a balance between flexibility and file size. Flexibility means the ability to go back and revise your work. In the previous project, the procedure gives priority to limiting the file size. If you wanted to go back and switch the positions of the Coit Tower and the bridge quadrants, you'd have to start from the beginning, because those pixels are no longer in the final work file—they were removed when you deleted them.

In this project, you'll give priority to flexibility. You'll apply a clipping path to combine one image with another. Your final work file will contain all the original pixel information, so that you can go back later and make adjustments whenever needed.

Arranging the image layers

A clipping path serves as a kind of cutting template for a layer. For example, text can be a clipping path, as if you glued an image onto the text and then dissolved all the areas of the image that weren't attached to the text characters. Transparent areas on the clipping path produce transparency on the image layer.

In this project, you're going to combine two views. You'll make the photograph of airplanes gradually fade into the picture of the bridge. You'll create the transition by using a clipping path that gradually flows from fully opaque to fully transparent pixels.

1   In the Organizer, press and hold the Ctrl key, and select the 08_04a and 08_04b files. Choose Edit > Go to Standard Edit to open the files in the Editor.

2   Choose Window > Images > Tile to view both images at the same time.

3   Select the Move tool (▶⊕). While holding down the Shift key, click and drag from the jet fighters window (08_04b) into the bridge window (08_04a). Release the mouse button when you see the dark outline around the bridge image, and then release the Shift key.

4   Close the 08_04b image window without saving the file.

5   In the Layers palette, select Layer 1 (jet fighters). Then choose Image > Resize > Scale.

6   In the tool options bar, type **65%** in the W (width) option, and then click Maintain Aspect Ratio (⬚). This scales the height by the same percentage.

7   Click the Commit button (✔) in the tool options bar to accept the changes.

8   Select the Move Tool then click and drag the planes on Layer 1 to the upper right corner so the planes are positioned half way between the horizon and the top of the image.

Adding a gradient layer

You'll create a gradient that will eventually be used to blend the layers together.

1   In the Layers palette, click New Layer (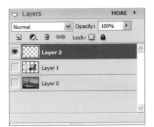) to create and select a new, blank layer named Layer 2.

2   In the toolbox, select the Gradient tool (▭), and then select the Default Foreground and Background Colors icon or press the D key on your keyboard.

3 In the tool options bar, click the arrow to open the Gradient Editor. Double-click to select the Foreground to Transparent thumbnail. Its name appears in a tooltip when you roll the mouse over it.

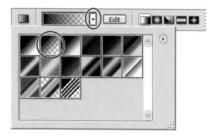

4 Make sure that the other settings in the tool options bar are as follows:

- Radial Gradient (■)

- Mode: Normal

- Opacity: 100%

- Transparency is selected

5 While holding down the Shift key, click and drag the Gradient tool horizontally to the right, beginning in the center of the middle jet and ending at the right edge of the image.

Applying the clipping path to a layer

With your gradient layer completed, it's time to put it to work.

1 In the Layers palette, drag the new gradient layer, Layer 2, under Layer 1, the jet fighters.

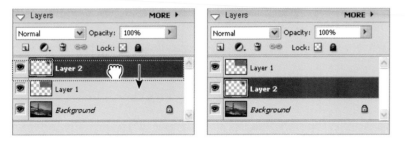

2 Select Layer 1, the top layer in the stack, and choose Layer > Group with Previous.

This action defines Layer 2 as the clipping path for Layer 1. In the Layers palette, Layer 1 is indented and shows an arrow pointing down to Layer 2.

3 Choose File > Save As.

4 In the Save As dialog box, name the file 08_04_Work, and save it in the My CIB Work folder, selecting Photoshop (PSD) for the Format. If the Photoshop Elements Format Options dialog box appears, keep Maximize Compatibility selected, and click OK.

Creating a clean edge with defringing

Defringing is used to remove that annoying bit of color that comes along when copying and pasting a part of an image or deleting a selected background. When the copied area is pasted down onto another background color, or the selected background is deleted, you can see a fine halo around your selection. Defringe blends the halo away so you won't see a hard line.

Now you'll composite an image of a family standing in front of the bridge by selecting and deleting the background and using the defringe feature.

1   Click the Photo Browser button to return to the Organizer, and open 08_04c.psd, the picture of the family, in Standard Edit mode.

2   Select the Move tool (⏵⊕). While holding down the Shift key, click and drag from the family image (08_04c.psd) into the bridge window (08_04a.psd). Release the mouse button when you see the dark outline around the bridge image, and release the Shift key.

3   Close the image 08_04c.psd.

4   In the Layers palette, select Layer 3, the family, then choose Image > Resize > Scale.

5   In the tool options bar, type **70%** in the W (width) option, and then click Maintain Aspect Ratio (⧉) to scale the height by the same percentage.

6   Click the Commit button (✔) in the tool options bar to accept the changes.

7   Select the Move tool. Click and drag Layer 3, the family, to the lower left corner of the bridge image.

8   Select the Magic Wand tool and click on the pink-colored background in the upper left corner of the family picture. Then while holding down the Shift key, click on any remaining pink areas to select the background.

9   Press the Delete key to delete the background and press Ctrl+D to deselect. You can also choose Select > Deselect.

10   Select the Zoom tool and zoom in on the bag that the woman on the left is carrying. The fringe is clearly visible.

11 Choose Enhance > Adjust Color and select Defringe Layer.

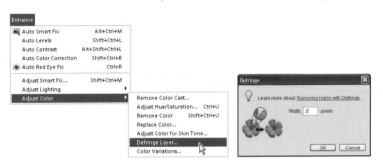

12 Enter **2** pixels for the width and click OK. Notice how the fringe is eliminated.

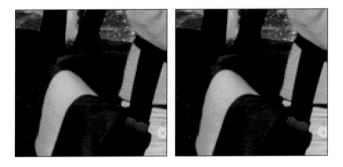

13 Double-click on the Hand tool in the toolbox to fit the image in the window.

14 Choose File > Save to save the file in your My CIB Work folder.

Congratulations, you've completed another project. In this one, you've learned how to create a composite image by arranging layers using a gradient layer as a clipping path. You also used the Defringe option, which eliminates the edge pixels that remain from a deleted background.

Review

▶ **Review questions**

1   What are some of the visual aids you can turn on to help you position items precisely in an image window?

2   How can you customize a grid or ruler?

3   Why is it when you think you're finished with a transformation that you cannot select another tool or perform other actions?

4   What is a clipping path and how do you create it? What are grouped layers?

5   How do you link two layers together?

▶ **Review answers**

1   Using the View menu, you can choose the Rulers and Grid commands to toggle them on and off. The rulers appear on the left and upper sides of the image window. The grid is superimposed on the image. Neither of these elements is a permanent part of the image, and neither appears when you print the image or save it in another format, such as JPEG.

2   You can customize grids and rulers using the Preferences dialog box. Choose Edit > Preferences > Units and Rulers or Edit > Preferences > Grid to access these options. You can also choose View > Snap to Grid. When selected, this command makes items snap into alignment with the nearest grid lines when you move them with the Move tool.

3   Photoshop Elements is waiting for your confirmation of the transformation by requiring you to click the Commit button in the tool options bar, or to double-click inside the transformation boundary.

4   Clipping paths and grouped layers are synonymous in Photoshop Elements 4.0. The lower of the two grouped layers must have areas of transparency. The other layer must be directly above it and must be selected. Choose Layer > Group with Previous to create the clipping path. When this is done, the transparent areas of the lower layer also apply to the upper layer. Effectively, the layer with the transparency serves as a cut-out form for the other layer—and that's its only function.

5   Start by selecting one layer, then Ctrl+click the layer to which you'd like to link. Click the link icon in the top of the Layers palette. You can also click the More button at the top right of the Layers palette and choose Link Layers.

9 Advanced Editing Techniques

In this lesson, you will discover how to take advantage of advanced editing techniques in Adobe Photoshop Elements. You will discover how to improve the quality and clarity of your images with advanced use of tools in Photoshop Elements. You will learn the following:

- Use camera raw images from your digital camera.

- Save conversions in the DNG format.

- Use histograms to understand the characteristics of an image.

- Understand highlights and shadows.

- Resize and sharpen an image.

- Create effects with the filter gallery.

- Use the cookie cutter.

Most users can complete this lesson in a little over an hour.

This lesson assumes that you are already familiar with the overall features of the Photoshop Elements 4.0 work area and recognize the two ways in which you can use Photoshop Elements: the Editor and the Organizer. If you need to learn more about these items, see Photoshop Elements Help and the Adobe Photoshop Elements 4.0 Getting Started Guide. This lesson also builds on the skills and concepts covered in the earlier lessons.

In this lesson, you will use the CIB Catalog you created earlier in the book. If necessary, open this catalog by choosing File > Catalog in Photo Organizer, then click Open

What is a raw image?

Unlike many of the other file names that you may know, such as JPEG, or GIF, raw files are referred to as such because they are unprocessed by the digital camera.

Whether you are a professional or amateur photographer, it can be difficult to understand all the process settings on your digital camera. Processing images incorrectly may degrade the quality of an image. One solution is to use the camera's raw setting. Raw images are derived directly from the camera's sensors, prior to any camera processing. Not all digital cameras offer the ability to shoot raw images, but many of the newer and more advanced cameras have this option.

Note: Raw files have different extensions depending upon the camera used to take the picture, such as Canon's .CRW and .CR2, Minolta's .MRW, Olympus' .ORF, and the various flavors of Nikon's .NEF.

You can open a raw file in Photoshop Elements, process it, and save it—instead of relying on the camera to process the file. Working with camera raw files lets you adjust proper white balance, tonal range, contrast, color saturation, and sharpening, after the image has been taken.

The benefits of a raw image

Raw images are high-quality image files that contain the maximum amount of original image data in a relatively small file size. Though larger than a compressed file, such as JPEG, raw images contain more data and take less space than a TIFF image.

Flexibility is another benefit, since many of the camera settings like sharpening, white balance, levels, and color adjustments can be undone when using Photoshop Elements. For instance, adjustments to exposure can be undone and recalculated based on the raw data. Also, because raw has 12 bits of available data, you are able to extract shadow and highlight detail which would have been lost in the 8 bits/channel JPEG or TIFF format.

Raw files provide an archival image format, much like a digital negative, but one that outlasts the usefulness and longevity of film. You can reprocess the file repeatedly to achieve the results you want. Photoshop Elements doesn't save your changes to the original raw file, rather it saves the last setting you used to process it.

Workflow overview

To use raw files, you need to set your camera to save files in its own raw file format. When you download the files from the camera. Photoshop Elements can open raw files only from the supported cameras listed on Adobe's Web site, www.adobe.com.

After processing the raw image file with the Camera Raw window, you open the image in Photoshop Elements, where you can work with it in the same way that you work with any photo. Then, you can save the file in any format supported by Photoshop Elements, such as PSD.

Note: *The RAW plug-in, which is used to open files from a digital camera, is updated over time as new cameras are supported. It may be necessary for you to replace your plug-in with the latest version from the www.adobe.com Web site.*

Getting started

Before you start working on files, take a few moments to make sure that your work area is set up for these projects.

1 Start Photoshop Elements in Standard Edit mode, either by selecting Edit and Enhance Photos in the Welcome Screen. If the Organizer is already open click the Edit button (▧) and choose Go to Standard Edit.

2   While in Standard Edit mode, choose File > Open. Navigate to the Lesson09 folder and open baby.CR2. The Camera Raw window appears.

Note: CR2 is the extension for a raw image generated from a Canon EOS Digital Rebel XT camera.

The camera raw window provides the tools that you need to make adjustments to your image.
A. Zoom tool. B. Hand tool. C. White Balance tool. D. Rotate counter-clockwise. E. Rotate clockwise. F. Shadows and Highlights. G. Histogram. H. Settings. I. Zoom level. J. Bit Depth.

3   Make sure that Preview is checked.

When you open a camera raw file, Photoshop Elements reads information in the file to see which model of camera created it, and then applies the appropriate camera settings to the image. You can select saved settings from the Settings drop-down menu. Later in this lesson you will learn how to save settings.

4   In the Settings drop-down menu, make sure that Camera Raw Defaults is selected.

💡 *You can save the current settings as the default for the camera that created the image by clicking the triangle next to the Settings menu and selecting Save New Camera Raw Defaults.*
You can also use the Photoshop Elements default settings for your camera, by clicking the triangle (▶)next to the Settings menu and selecting Reset Camera Raw Defaults.

There are two palettes in the Camera Raw window: Adjust and Detail.

The Adjust palette gives you the controls to fine-tune using options not available within the standard edit tools in Photoshop Elements. The Detail palette gives you controls to adjust sharpening and noise. You will use the controls on the Adjust palette.

Note: *Any correction you make to an image removes data from that image. Because you are working with much more information in a RAW file, any changes you make to the settings, such as exposure and white balance, will have less impact on the image than if you made drastic changes in a .PSD, TIFF, or JPEG file.*

Camera raw controls

Zoom tool—Sets the preview zoom to the next preset zoom value when you click in the preview image. Alt+click to set the next lower zoom value. Drag the Zoom tool in the preview image to zoom in on a selected area. To return to 100%, double-click the Zoom tool.

Hand tool—Moves the image in the preview window if the preview image is set at a zoom level higher than 100%. Hold down the spacebar to access the Hand tool while using another tool. Double-click the Hand tool to fit the preview image in the window.

White Balance tool—Sets the area you click to a neutral gray tone to remove color casts and adjust the color of the entire image. The Temperature and Tint values change to reflect the color adjustment.

Rotate buttons—Rotates the photo either counterclockwise or clockwise.

Shadow and **Highlight**—Turn on the display of shadow and highlight clipping. Clipped shadows appear in blue, and clipped highlights appear in red.

Note: Clipped highlights are highlight areas that are uniformly white with no detail. Likewise, clipped shadows are shadow areas that are uniformly black with no detail.

RGB—Indicates the Red, Green, and Blue values of the pixel directly below the cursor as you move it over the preview image. The values display when you are using either the Zoom tool, Hand tool, or the White Balance eyedropper.

Depth—Specifies whether the image opens as 8 or 16 bits per color channel.

Settings Options—in this menu set or reset color, lighting, sharpening, and noise settings to the image based on another image or the camera's default settings. Choose from the following options:

> **Image Settings**—restores the settings of the current image to their values at the time you first opened the Camera Raw dialog box.
>
> **Camera Default**—applies the default camera raw settings.
>
> **Previous Conversion**—applies the setting used for the last camera raw image you processed.
>
> **Custom**—is automatically chosen when one of the sliders is adjusted. It allows you to work with an image without using any presets.

—From Photoshop Elements Help

5 In the Adjust palette, experiment by trying some of the presets available in the White Balance drop down menu.

Presets are helpful if you need to accommodate for color casts introduced by poor lighting conditions when the image was taken. For example, if your camera was not set up correctly to deal with a cloudy day, you can fix it here by selecting Cloudy from the White Balance drop-down window.

Notice the change in the preview window as you select various White Balance presets. In the next section you will discover why selecting the correct white balance is very important to the overall look of the image.

6   Before moving to the next part of this lesson, select As Shot from the White Balance drop-down menu.

Adjusting the white balance

In this lesson you are going to adjust the white balance by locating a neutral and selecting it with the White Balance tool. Neutral colors include black, white, and gray. By understanding what a neutral is and how it works, you can easily and quickly remove color tints from an image in the Raw window.

1   Make sure that the Auto checkboxes for Exposure, Shadows, Brightness, Contrast and Saturation are unchecked.

2   Select the White Balance tool (⚲) from the tools at the top of the Camera Raw window.

3   Locate a neutral in the image. A good example of a neutral in the image is the tag in the lower left of the image. Click on the white area in the middle of the tag.

Unbalanced image.   *Balanced image.*

The White Balance is now at Custom and the image is balanced.

Using the White Balance tool accurately removes any color cast, or tint, from an image. Depending upon the subject matter, you might want a slight controlled color tint. In this instance you will warm up the image using the Temperature and Tint controls.

4   Click on the Temperature slider. Temperature controls the blue-yellow balance. Either click and drag the slider slightly to the right, or press the arrow up key (↑) to increase the color temperature 50 Kelvin increments at a time. This is a visual adjustment, so adjust until you add just a touch of yellow to the image. We moved the slider to 4850.

What is color temperature?

The term color temperature derives from the position of a color along a continuum from warm (red) to cool (blue). It is the degree of heat (in Kelvin) that an object would have to absorb before it glowed in a certain color. Each color is associated with a color temperature, as are various kinds of light.

The Tint allows you to adjust the red and green balance. You will add a slight amount of red to this image.

5   Drag the Tint slider to the left to increase the red. We dragged the slider to -30. Leave the image open for the next part of this lesson.

Use Tint and Temperature to adjust the color tint of an image. Your values may differ slightly than those shown.

Using the tone controls

Tonal controls are located under the White Balance controls in the raw window. In this next section, you find out how to use the tone controls to adjust for incorrect exposure as well as check shadows, adjust brightness, contrast, and saturation.

Before you make adjustments, make certain you understand these essential items:

Exposure is a measure of the amount of light in which a photo was taken. Underexposed digital photos are too dark; overexposed ones, too light. Use this control to recover the lighter, or blown-out, information from overexposed images.

Shadows are the darkest elements in an image. Use this control to darken the shadows in an image.

Brightness controls the relative lightness or darkness of an image and the colors in the image.

Contrast is the difference in brightness between light and dark areas of an image. Contrast determines the number of shades in the image. An image without contrast can appear "washed out." An image with too much contrast can lose the smooth gradation of one shade of color to the next.

Saturation is the purity, or strength, of a color. Also called chroma. A fully saturated color contains no gray. Saturation controls make colors more vivid (less black or white added) or more muted (more black or white added).

You will check the Exposure of this image and make adjustments based upon the lightness values in this image.

Adjusting the exposure

If there is detail to be found in an overexposed image, adjusting the Exposure slider will helps to recover it. Before you adjust the exposure, you should understand two terms: Specular highlights and clipping.

Specular highlights Specular highlights are areas of an image that should be pure white. Examples of specular highlights are: the chrome of a car bumper, the reflection on shiny jewelry, the flame of a candle, or in this image, the reflection on the buckle of the overalls. These specular highlights should remain bright white to add impact and allow the rest of the image a better tonal range. Pure white on an image is generally reserved for specular highlights.

This jewelry has many reflective areas.   *The reflection on the buckle is a specular highlight.*

Clipping can make the highlights more white and shadows more black. This can be done in the highlight and shadows of an image. In most cases, some clipping can be helpful, but too much clipping eliminates valuable information.

You will now adjust the Exposure and Shadow sliders. By moving the sliders to the left or right you can adjust the exposure of an image.

1 Hold down the Alt key while moving the Exposure slider. This shows the clipping (what will be forced to white) as you adjust the exposure. We moved the slider to -0.60.

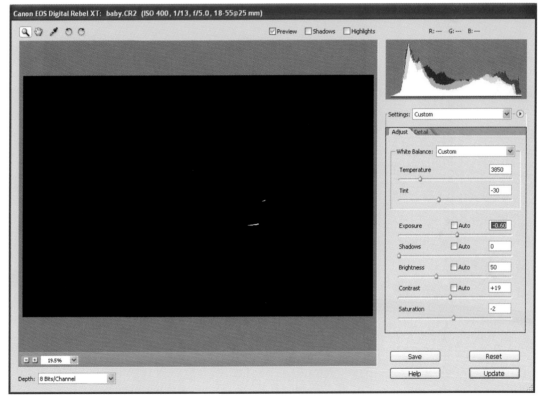

Hold down the Alt key while sliding the Exposure to see highlight clipping.

Now you will adjust the shadow.

2   Hold down the Alt key and click and drag the Shadow slider. Any areas that appear in the clipping preview will be forced to a solid black. Release when only the deep areas of shadow in the image appear as black. If a large amount of the pupils of the eye appear you have made too much of an adjustment. The image will lose detail in the fabric behind the baby if you push the shadow too far. We moved the slider to 3.

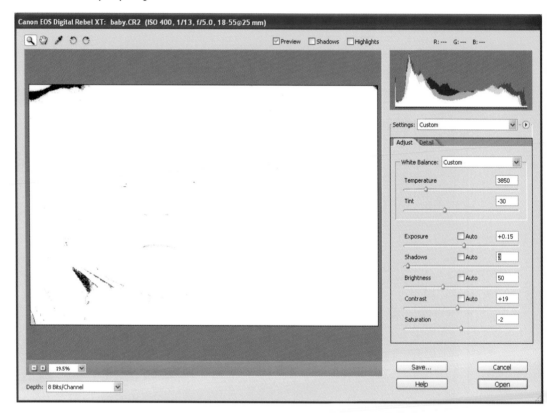

3   Select the Brightness slider and press the up arrow on the keyboard to increase the value to 55.

4   Select the Contrast slider and press the up arrow key on the keyboard to increase the value to +30.

5   Leave the Saturation slider untouched.

💡 *For an interesting effect you can drag the Saturation slider all the way to the left to neutralize your image, essentially creating a three-color grayscale.*

Saving the image

You can reprocess this raw file repeatedly to achieve the results you want by saving in the DNG format. Photoshop Elements doesn't save your changes to the original raw file, but it saves the last setting you used to process it.

The DNG format

Raw file formats are becoming extremely popular in digital photography. However, each camera manufacturer has their own proprietary raw format. This means that not every raw file can be read by software other than the one provided with the camera. This may make it difficult to use these images in the future, as the camera manufacturer may not support the file format indefinitely. This is also a problem if you want to use software other than what was supplied by the camera manufacturer.

To help alleviate these problems, you can save raw images from Photoshop Elements in the DNG format, a publicly available archival format for the raw files generated by digital cameras. The DNG format provides an open standard for the files created by individual camera models, and helps to ensure that you will be able to access your files in the future.

1   In the baby.CR2 raw window click Save. The Save Options window appears.

2   With Save in New Location selected in the Destination drop-down menu, click on the Select Folder button and navigate to your My CIB Work folder.

3 In the File Naming section, leave the name in the drop-down menu on the left side unchanged. Click the drop-down menu on the right and select 2 Digit Serial Number. This puts the numbers 01 following the name.

4 Click Save. The file along with the present settings has been saved as a DNG file, using a format which you can retrieve repeatedly.

5 The Save Options window closes and the raw window is displayed again. Click the Open button.

The baby.CR2 file opens in Photoshop Elements. Now you can work with this file the same way that you work with any photo.

6 Choose File > Save. Navigate to the My CIB Work folder. Name the file **baby_ edited-work.psd**. Make sure the selection in the Format drop-down menu is Photoshop. Click Save.

7 Choose File > Close.

Using histograms

Many of your images may be saved using a variety of formats, including JPEG, TIFF, or PSD. For these images you will make your adjustments in the Standard Editor. In this part of the lesson, you will discover how to use the histogram to understand what changes can be made to your images to improve their quality.

In this section, you will open an image that was shot with poor lighting, and also has a slight magenta cast to it. Many digital cameras introduce a slight cast into images.

What is a histogram?

The Histogram palette, located under Window > Histogram, shows whether the image contains enough detail in the shadows, midtones, and highlights. A histogram also helps you recognize where changes need to be made in the image.

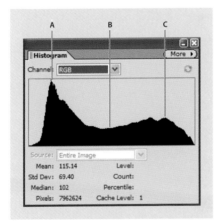

Histograms show detail and tonal range of an image.
A. *Shadows.* **B**. *Midtones.* **C**. *Highlights.*

Tonal corrections, such as lightening an image, remove information from the image. Excessive correction is recognizable by the viewer, and causes posterization, or banding in the image.

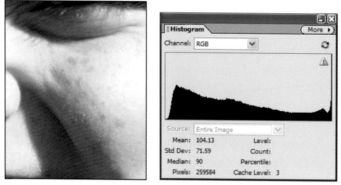

This histogram shows the detail necessary to make corrections.

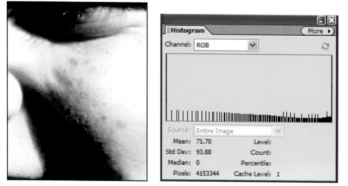

This histogram reveals that this image is already lacking detail. Additional corrections will degrade the image even more.

Understanding highlights and shadows

In the next part of this lesson, you will open an image and adjust the highlight and shadow. You will also make additional tonal corrections while keeping an eye on the Histogram palette.

1   Return to the Organizer by clicking on the Photo Browser button in the shortcuts bar in the Standard Editor.

2   Select Edit > Preferences > General and make sure that Show File Names in Details is checked.

3   Go to the Organizer, select the file face.psd and choose Edit > Go to Standard Edit. The image is tagged with the Lesson9 tag to make it easy to locate. Notice the image is a little dark.

4   Choose File > Save As and navigate to the My CIB Work folder. Save the image as **face_work.psd**. Click Save.

5   If it is not visible choose Window > Histogram.

This image needs more information in the lighter areas of the image.

According to the Histogram palette, the vast amount of the data in this image is located in the middle (midtones) of the image and the left (shadow). You will open the tonal range of this image using Levels.

6   Choose Enhance > Adjust Lighting > Levels. The Levels window appears.

You will use the shadow, midtone, and highlight sliders, as well as the Set Black Point, Set Gray Point, and Set White Point eyedroppers in this exercise.

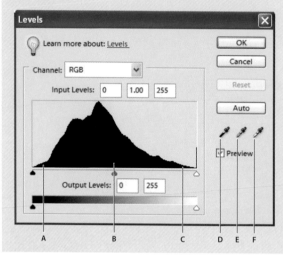

The Levels window.
*A. Shadow. **B**. Midtone. **C**. Highlight. **D**. Set Black Point.*
*E. Set Gray Point. **F**. Set White Point.*

7   Double-click on the Set White Point eyedropper. This opens the Color Picker. In this window, you will choose the highlight of your image. You will designate the lightest, non-specular, point in the image as being the highlight.

8   Type **240** in the R (Red), G (Green), and B (Blue) text fields. This defines the light point of your image as a light gray, not pure white. Pure white is reserved for specular highlights in an image. Click OK in the Color Picker window.

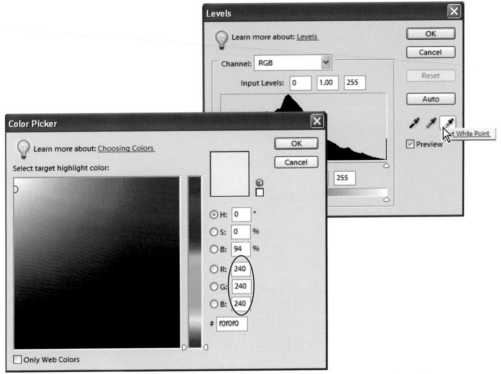

Double-click on the Set White Point eyedropper to change the highlight value in the Color Picker.

9 Hold down the Alt key and click on the Highlight slider. The clipping preview for the highlight appears. The visible areas are the lightest area of the image. Release the Alt key to see you've located the lightest portion of the sweater in the image.

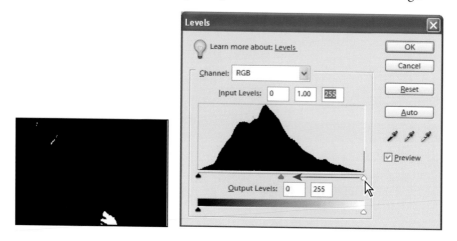

10 Select the Set White Point eyedropper and click on the location of your image (light part of the sweater) that appeared in the clipping preview.

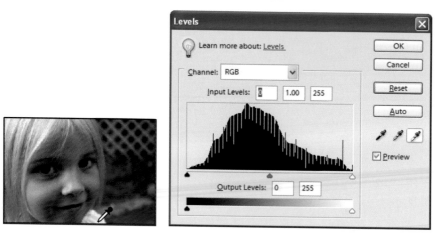

You will now set the Shadow area using a slightly different technique.

11 Hold down the Alt key and click then drag the shadow slider to the right until the eyes, or darkest area of the image, appear as dark spots in the shadow clipping preview.

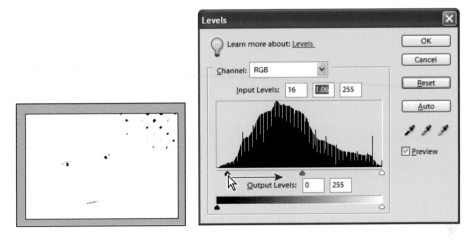

12 Adjust the midtone visually by selecting the midtone slider (middle) and dragging it to the left. This is lightens the midtones. Watch the Histogram palette as you make this change to see the old data (displayed as gray) compared to the correction that you are now making (displayed as black). We adjusted our midtone to 1.56.

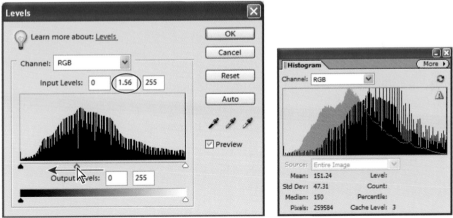

Adjust the midtones.   *Watch change in Histogram palette.*

Some gaps will be created, but you want to avoid creating very large gaps. Even if the image looks fine on screen, large gaps may cause a loss of data that is visible when printed.

Using Set Gray Point

If you have a neutral in your image, you can remove a color cast quickly using the Set Gray Point dropper. Neutrals are pixels in the white to black range, preferably more toward gray.

1   Select the Set Gray Point eyedropper in the Levels window and click on a neutral gray in the image. In this case, click on any part of the road in the background. Any color cast is removed.

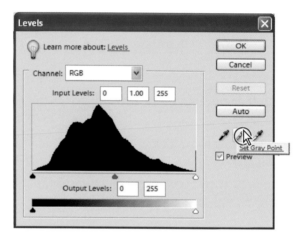

Note: You do not want to remove color cast from every image. You may want some images to be warmer or cooler for a visual effect.

2   Click OK. When the Adobe Photoshop Elements alert window appears, click Yes. You want to save the new target colors so you do not have to set the white point every time you use the Levels window to make adjustments.

3   Select Edit > Undo Levels or press Ctrl+Z to see how the image looked prior to changing the highlights and shadows. Choose Edit > Redo Levels or Press Ctrl+Y to bring back the correction you made.

Leave this image open for the next part of this lesson.

Unsharp mask

Here you will add some crispness to your image and make it "pop" when printed. Using the sharpening tools correctly can have a significant impact on your image.

Image with no sharpening.   *Image with unsharp mask applied.*

You'll use the Unsharp mask feature in Photoshop Elements. How can something be unsharp and yet sharpen an image? The term unsharp mask has it roots in the print production industry: the technique was implemented by making an out-of-focus negative film—the unsharp mask—and then printing the original in a sandwich with this negative film. This produces a halo around the edges of objects – giving them more definition.

💡 *If you are planning to resize an image, resize first then apply the Unsharp mask filter.*

1   With the face_work.psd image still open, choose Image > Resize > Image Size. This image needs to be made smaller, but with a higher resolution (pixels per inch).

2   If necessary, uncheck the Resample Image checkbox at the bottom of the window, and type **300** into the Resolution text field. Notice that the width and height increments adjust. This method to increases the resolution in the image without losing information. Resolution is the fineness of detail you can see in an image. It is measured in pixels per inch (ppi). The more pixels per inch, the greater the resolution. Generally, the higher the resolution of your image, the better the printed image quality.

3 Re-check Resample image to reduce the height and width of the image and not affect the resolution. Type **3** into the width text field. In this case, we are throwing away the data that we do not need for a larger image. Click OK.

Always resize before sharpening an image.

4 Choose File > Save. Keep the file open for the next part of this lesson.

Applying the Unsharp Mask filter

Before applying any filter in Adobe Photoshop Elements, it is best to be at 100% view.

1 With the face_work.psd image still open, choose View > Actual pixels.

2 Choose Filter > Sharpen > Unsharp Mask. The Unsharp Mask window appears.

The amount of unsharp masking you apply is determined by the subject matter. A portrait, such as this image, should be softer than an image of an object such as an automobile. The adjustments range from 100 to 500, with 500 being the sharpest.

3 Slide the Amount adjustment or type **100** in the Adjustment text field.

Disable the preview in the Unsharp Mask window by clicking and holding down on the preview pane. When you release the mouse, the preview is enabled again. To reveal other portions of the image click and drag in the preview pane.

4   Leave the Radius at 1 pixel, but change the Threshold to 10 pixels. Threshold is a
key control in this window, as it tells the filter what not to sharpen, In this case the value
10 tells it to not sharpen a pixel if it is within 10 shades of the pixel next to it.

5   Click OK and choose File > Save, then choose File > Close.

Create effects with the filter gallery

You can experiment and apply interesting filter effects using the Filter Gallery. The Filter Gallery allows you to apply multiple filters at the same time, as well as re-arrange the order in which they affect the image.

1 In the Organizer select the file named blues.psd and choose Edit > Go to Standard Edit from the shortcuts bar.

2 Choose File > Save and navigate to the My CIB Work folder. Name the file **blues_work.psd**.

Because many filters use the active foreground and background colors to create effects, take a moment and set them now.

3 Click on the Default Foreground and Background Color swatches at the bottom of the toolbar. This resets the default black foreground and white background colors.

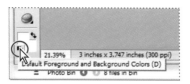

4 Choose Filter > Filter Gallery. The Filter Gallery window appears.

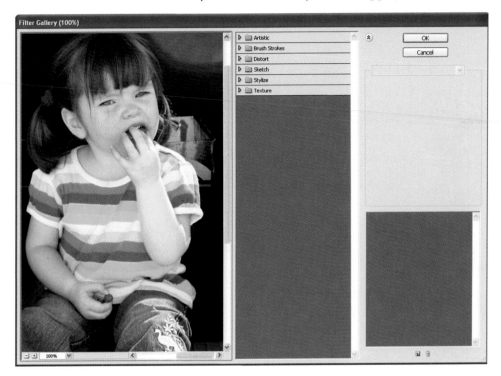

5 Click and hold on the mouse to temporarily change the cursor into the hand tool (🖑) in the preview pane. While holding the mouse down, drag the image so that you can see the image of a girl in the preview pane.

Note: It is important to view images at 100% view to see accurate results.

Listed in the Filter Gallery are several categories of filters from which you can choose.

6 Expand the Artistic category by clicking on the arrow to the left of Artistic.

7 Select Palette Knife. The filter is applied in the preview image.

8 Using the Stroke Size slider, change the value to 7.

9 Click the New Effect layer (▣) on the bottom right, then select Dry Brush from the Artistic filters. Both the Palette Knife and Dry Brush filters are applied simultaneously.

10 Click on the New Effect layer again. This time, expand the Distort filters and select Diffuse Glow.

11   Using the Glow amount slider, change the value to 2.

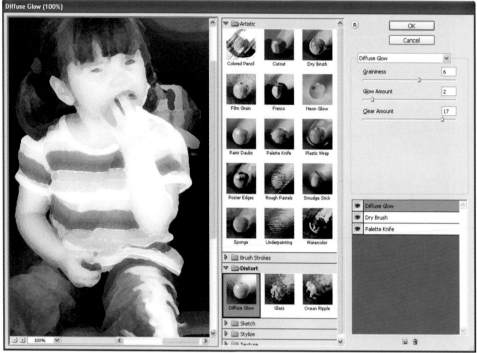

The Filter Gallery allows you to apply multiple filters simultaneously.

Note: *You can read more details about what each filter does in "About filters" in Adobe Photoshop Elements Help.*

Experimenting with filters in the gallery

Experiment with the three filters that you have applied by turning off the visibility of selected filters or rearranging their placement in the gallery.

1   Turn off a Dry Brush filter in the Filter Gallery by clicking on the eye icon (👁) to the left of the Dry Brush.

2 Re-arrange the filters by clicking and dragging the Palette Knife filter to the top of the list.

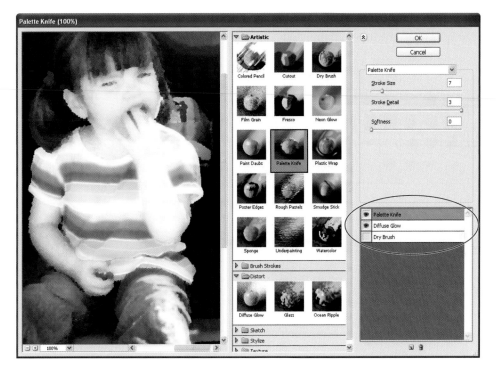

3 Click OK to close the Filter Gallery window and apply the changes.

4 Choose File > Save. Keep this file open for the next part of the lesson.

Using the Cookie Cutter tool

The Cookie Cutter tool allows you to crop an image into a shape that you choose.

Use the Cookie Cutter tool to clip a photo into a fun or interesting shape. In this part of the lesson, you'll add a rough edge to the image.

1 Select the Cookie Cutter tool from the tool box.

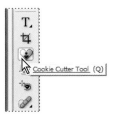

2   Click the Shapes menu on the tool options bar to view a library of shapes from which you can select. The visible selections are the default shapes.

3   Click and hold the triangle (⊙) on the right side of the shapes library. Choose Crop Shapes from the list that appears.

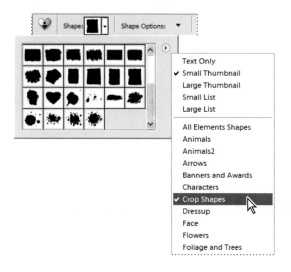

Note: The assigned names for each of the shapes appears as a tooltip when you cross over it.

4   Select the shape Crop Shape 30.

5   Click and drag to create the shape on the image. Use the handles to scale the crop.

Set Shape Options:

Unconstrained—Draws the shape to any size or dimension you'd like.

Defined Proportions—Keeps the height and width of the cropped shape in proportion.

Defined Size—Crops the photo to the exact size of the shape you chose.

Fixed Size—Specifies exact measurements for the finished shape.

From Center—Draws the shape from the center.

Enter a value for **Feather** to soften the edges of the finished shape.

Note: Feathering softens the edges of the cropped image so that the edges fade out and blend in with the background.

—From Adobe Photoshop Elements Help

6   Click the Commit button (✔) located in the tool options bar, or press Enter to finish the cropping. If you want to cancel the cropping operation, click the Cancel button (◯) or press the Esc key.

7   Choose File > Save. Then choose File > Close.

Congratulations, you have finished the lesson on advanced editing techniques in Adobe Photoshop Elements. You discovered how to take advantage of the raw features and adjust images using the histogram as a reference. You also found out how to make playful frames using the Cookie Cutter tool.

Exploring on your own

1   Review the raw feature in Adobe Photoshop Elements by opening the file named farm.CR2. Experiment with the tint and temperature to create a better image

2   Open the file named read.psd and practice adjusting the highlight and shadow using the Levels window.

3   Open any image; if you do not have one you would like to use, open pumpkin.psd from the Lesson09 folder. Use the Cookie Cutter tool and select a shape. Don't forget that you have additional choices in the library.

When you have applied a cookie cutter crop, experiment with some effects. Choose Window > Styles and Effects. Experiment with different beveled edges and drop shadows to create interesting effects to your crop. Read more about the Styles and Effects in Adobe Photoshop Elements Help "About filters, effects, and layer styles."

Learning more

We hope you've gained confidence, skill, and knowledge about how to use Photoshop Elements for your digital photography work. But this book is just the start. You can learn even more by studying the Photoshop Elements 4.0 Help system, which is built into the application by choosing Help > Photoshop Elements Help. Also, don't forget to look for tutorials, tips, and expert advice on the Adobe Web site, www.adobe.com.

Review

▶ **Review questions**

1   What is a camera raw image, and what are three benefits to using it?

2   What different methods can you use to control the white balance in the raw window?

3   What tools can you use in the Levels control to set highlight and shadow?

4   What is the Cookie Cutter tool used for?

▶ **Review answers**

1   A raw file is one that is unprocessed by a digital camera. Not a cameras create raw files.

Benefits include the following:

Flexibility—many of the camera settings, such as sharpening, white balance, levels and color adjustments can be undone when using Photoshop Elements.

Quality—because RAW has 12 bits of available data, you are able to extract shadow and highlight detail which would have been lost in a 8 bits/channel JPEG or TIFF format.

Archive—RAW files provide an archival image format, much like a digital negative, but one that outlasts the usefulness and longevity of film. You can reprocess the file repeatedly to achieve the results you want.

2   Three methods to control the White balance in the Raw window include:

• You can set the white balance in an image automatically by using the White Balance eyedropper tool in the raw window. By selecting the White Balance eyedropper and clicking on a neutral, the Temperature and Tint sliders are automatically adjusted.

• Another method is to select a preset white balance from the White Balance drop-down menu. Here you can choose from options that include corrections based upon whether the flash was used, it was a cloudy day, or the image was shot in fluorescent light, to name a few.

- You can also manually change the Temperature and Tint adjustments by using the appropriate sliders under White Balance.

3   Use the Set Black Point and Set White Point eyedropper tools in the Levels window.

- In the Levels window you can double-click on the Set Black Point and Set White Point tools to enter the desired values.

- To find the light point, you can Alt+drag the shadow or highlight slider. This turns on the clipping preview.

- Select the darkest point with the Set Black Point tool by selecting the tool and clicking on the darkest part of the image.

- Select the lightest point by using the Set White Point tool to click on the lightest part of the image.

4   The Cookie Cutter tool is used to clip an image in a variety of shapes. Use the default shapes in the Shape drop-down menu, or select from a variety of libraries available in the Shape window's palette.

Index

A

ACTP 9
Add Blank Slide button 111
Add Media button 108
Add to Selection 177, 181, 274
Add To Selection tool 201
Adjust Lighting 170
Adjust Lighting menu 170
adjustment layers 175, 192
 applying to a limited area 177
 comparing results 179
 Hue/Saturation 178
Adjust palette 301, 302
Adobe Acrobat Reader 9
Adobe Certified Expert (ACE) 9
Adobe Certified Training Providers (ACTP) 9
Adobe Photo Downloader 18
Adobe Photoshop Elements 4.0
 Installing 3
Adobe Photoshop Elements Help.
 See Help
Adobe Photoshop Services 79
Adobe Web site 9
Advanced Blending 205
Advanced Mode 48
anchor 279
anchor point 182, 230
Apply New Tag dialog box 71
ASF 28, 34
Aspect Ratio 277
Auto-fixing 120
auto adjustments 123
Auto Color 120, 163
Auto Contrast 120, 163
Auto Levels 120, 163
automatically tile 127
automatic correction 126
automatic fixes 162
Auto Red Eye Fix 133
Auto Smart Fix 58, 133
AVI 28, 34

B

Background Brush tool 199, 200
Background layer
 duplicate 164
Back to All Photos button 59
balance 176
batch 19, 41, 120
Before and After 123
bit depth 300, 302
blemishes, removing 223
blending mode 165, 167
 Multiply 167
 Normal 208, 290
 Overlay 168, 187
 Screen 165
Blur tool 211, 212, 221
book files
 copying 3
border 226
 Adding an uneven 229
 decorative 230
 quick 231
brightness 170, 306, 308
Brightness/Contrast window 170, 176
Bringing objects forward.
 See layers
brush 208
Brushed Aluminum Frame 230
Brush Size menu 199
Burn/Backup wizard 85
Burn to Disk 112, 114
Burn tool 220

C

calendar 249
calibration 157
camera 15
Camera Default 302
camera raw
 benefits 298
 controls 302
canvas 197
Canvas Size dialog box 229, 279

capture
 video 28
capture frames 28
capturing media 34
card reader 15, 45
cartoon balloons 236
 adding text 240
 drawing 237
cast 304
catalog
 adding unmanaged files 65
 creating 4, 16, 38
 importing attached tags 6
 reconnecting missing files 7
categories
 applying and editing 67
 converting 69
 creating 66
 hierarchy 69
 sub-categories 66
CD or DVD 34
 burning 85
certification 9
Chambers, Jeff 48
choosing files 24
Clear Emboss effect 247
Clear Layer Style 254
clipping 317
clipping layer 287
clipping path 291
Clone Stamp tool 218
Color 124
color cast 304
color correction 126
color management 156
 Allow Me to Choose setting 157
 Always Optimize for Computer Screens setting 157
 Always Optimize for Printing setting 157
 No Color Management setting 157
 setting up 157
Color Replacement tool 135, 158
Color Settings 157
color temperature 304
color values 171

tool options bar 181
transitions 102
  Random 103
  Wipe 103
transparency 287
tripod 196
Type tool 251

U

underexposed 175, 305
  brightening 163
  correcting with blending
      modes 185
Unsharp Mask 320
untagged 62

V

Vanishing Point 207
Vanishing Point tool 207
VCD 114
Version Set 86
Version sets 58
video
  acquiring still frames 28
video format support 28
viewing and finding photos 61
viewing modes 127
viewing photos 23

W

warping
  text 251
watched folders 49
Web browsers 247
Welcome Screen 16
white balance 305
White Point eyedropper 316
Windows Explorer
  dragging files from 39
Windows media center edition
      114
Windows XP Media Center 114
WMV 28, 34
work files 72
workflow 15
workspaces 11
  Editor 14
wrinkles, fixing 208
wrinkles and spots

removing 207

X

XP Media Center 114

Z

zoom 137
Zoom All Windows 174
Zoom tool 174, 182, 199, 216,
      302

Production Notes

The *Adobe Photoshop Elements 4.0 Classroom in a Book* was created electronically using Adobe InDesign CS2. Additional art was produced using Adobe Illustrator CS2, Adobe Photoshop CS2, and Adobe Photoshop Elements 4.0.

Team credits

The following individuals contributed to the development of new and updated lessons for this edition of the *Adobe Photoshop Elements Classroom in a Book*:

Project Manager: Christopher Smith

Technical writing: Greg Heald, Jennifer Smith, Jerron Smith, Greg Urbaniak

Production: AGI Training: Elizabeth Chambers

Artwork production: Lisa Fridsma

Proofreading: Jay Donahue

Technical Editors: Joda Alian, Cathy Auclair, Sean McKnight, Eric Rowse

Typefaces used

Set in the Adobe Minion Pro and Adobe Myriad Pro OpenType families of typefaces. More information about OpenType and Adobe fonts is available at Adobe.com.

Photo Credits

Photos supplied by Christopher Smith, Jennifer Smith, Greg Heald. Photos are for use only with the lessons in the book.